Can Human Rights Survive?

In this set of essays, originally presented as the 2005 Hamlyn Lectures, Conor Gearty considers whether human rights can survive the challenges of the war on terror, the revival of political religion, and the steady erosion of the world's natural resources. He also looks deeper than this to consider some fundamental questions: What are human rights? How can we tell what they are? Why should we believe in their existence? In his first essay, Gearty asks how the idea of human rights needs to be made to work in our age of relativism, uncertainty and anxiety. In the second, he assesses the dangers inherent in the legalisation of rights generally, and in particular how the idea of human rights has coped with its incorporation in legal form in the UK Human Rights Act, arguing that the British record is much better and more democratic than many human rights enthusiasts allow. In his final essay, Gearty confronts the challenge that may destroy the language of human rights for the generations that follow us: the bogus war on terror.
This book will appeal to everyone concerned with the global challenges to human rights today.

CONOR GEARTY is Rausing Director of the Centre for the Study of Human Rights and Professor of Human Rights Law at the London School of Economics and Political Science. He is a founding member of Matrix Chambers in London.

CAN HUMAN RIGHTS SURVIVE?

CONOR GEARTY

CAMBRIDGE
UNIVERSITY PRESS

CAMBRIDGE UNIVERSITY PRESS
Cambridge, New York, Melbourne, Madrid, Cape Town, Singapore,
São Paulo, Delhi, Dubai, Tokyo, Mexico City

Cambridge University Uress
The Edinburgh Building, Cambridge CB2 2RU, UK

www.cambridge.org
Information on this title: www.cambridge.org/9780521685528

First published 2006
Reprinted 2009, 2010

Printed in the United Kingdom at the University Press, Cambridge

A catalogue record for this publication is available from the British Library

ISBN 978-0-521-86644-6 Hardback
ISBN 978-0-521-68552-4 Paperback

CONTENTS

v

The Hamlyn Trust owes its existence today to the will of the late Miss Emma Warburton Hamlyn of Torquay, who died in 1941 at the age of 80. She came of an old and well-known Devon family. Her father, William Bussell Hamlyn, practised in Torquay as a solicitor and J.P. for many years, and it seems likely that Miss Hamlyn founded the trust in his memory. Emma Hamlyn was a woman of strong character, intelligent and cultured, well-versed in literature, music and art, and a lover of her country. She travelled extensively in Europe and Egypt, and apparently took considerable interest in the law and ethnology of the countries and cultures that she visited. An account of Miss Hamlyn by Professor Chantal Stebbings of the University of Exeter may be found, under the title 'The Hamlyn Legacy', in volume 42 of the published lectures.

Miss Hamlyn bequeathed the residue of her estate on trust in terms which it seems were her own. The wording was thought to be vague, and the will was taken to the Chancery Division of the High Court, which in November 1948 approved a Scheme for the administration of the trust. Paragraph 3 of the Scheme, which follows Miss Hamlyn's own wording, is as follows:

> The object of the charity is the furtherance by lectures or otherwise among the Common People of the United Kingdom of Great Britain and Northern Ireland of the

knowledge of the Comparative Jurisprudence and
Ethnology of the Chief European countries including the
United Kingdom, and the circumstances of the growth of
such jurisprudence to the Intent that the Common People
of the United Kingdom may realise the privileges which in
law and custom they enjoy in comparison with other
European Peoples and realising and appreciating such
privileges may recognise the responsibilities and
obligations attaching to them.

The Trustees are to include the Vice-Chancellor of the University
of Exeter, representatives of the Universities of London, Leeds,
Glasgow, Belfast and Wales and persons co-opted. At present
there are eight Trustees:

Professor N. Burrows, The University of Glasgow
Ms Clare Dyer
Professor K.M. Economides [representing the Vice-Chancellor
   of the University of Exeter] (Chairman)
Professor J. Morison, Queen's University, Belfast
The Rt Hon. Lord Justice Sedley
Professor A. Sherr, University of London
Professor P.A. Thomas, Cardiff University
Professor C. Walker, University of Leeds
Clerk: Ms Anna Hamlyn, University of Exeter

From the outset it was decided that the objects of the Trust
could be best achieved by means of an annual course of public
lectures of outstanding interest and quality by eminent lectur-
ers, and by their subsequent publication and distribution to
a wider audience. The first of the Lectures were delivered by

the Rt Hon. Lord Justice Denning (as he then was) in
1949. Since then there has been an unbroken series of annual
Lectures published by Sweet & Maxwell that from 2006 are to
be published by Cambridge University Press. A complete list of
the Lectures may be found on pages ix to xii. In 2005 the
Trustees decided to supplement the Lectures with an annual
Hamlyn Seminar, normally held at the Institute of Advanced
Legal Studies in the University of London, to mark the publication of the Lectures in printed book form. The Trustees have
also, from time to time, provided financial support for a
variety of projects which, in various ways, have disseminated
knowledge or have promoted a wider public understanding
of the law.

This, the 57th series of lectures was delivered by Pro-
fessor Conor Gearty at the London School of Economics and
Political Science, Durham University and the Queen's
University, Belfast during November 2005. The Board of
Trustees would like to record its appreciation to Professor
Gearty and also the three human rights centres based in these
three universities, which generously hosted the Lectures.

January 2006   KIM ECONOMIDES
                                  Chairman of the Trustees

1982 The Quest for Security: Employees, Tenants, Wives by Professor Tony Honoré
1983 Hamlyn Revisited: The British Legal System Today by Lord Hailsham of St Marylebone
1984 The Development of Consumer Law and Policy – Bold Spirits and Timorous Souls by Sir Gordon Borrie
1985 Law and Order by Professor Ralf Dahrendorf
1986 The Fabric of English Civil Justice by Sir Jack Jacob
1987 Pragmatism and Theory in English Law by P.S. Atiyah
1988 Justification and Excuse in the Criminal Law by J.C. Smith
1989 Protection of the Public – A New Challenge by the Rt Hon. Lord Justice Woolf
1990 The United Kingdom and Human Rights by Dr Claire Palley
1991 Introducing a European Legal Order by Sir Gordon Slynn
1992 Speech & Respect by Professor Richard Abel
1993 The Administration of Justice by Lord Mackay of Clashfern
1994 Blackstone's Tower: The English Law School by Professor William Twining
1995 From the Test Tube to the Coffin: Choice and Regulation in Private Life by the Hon. Mrs Justice Hale
1996 Turning Points of the Common Law by the Rt Hon. Lord Cooke of Thorndon
1997 Commercial Law in the Next Millennium by Professor Roy Goode
1998 Freedom Law and Justice by the Rt Hon. Lord Justice Sedley

ACKNOWLEDGEMENTS

I am grateful to the Hamlyn trustees for inviting me to give
the 2005 lectures, and for their kindness and efficiency in
making arrangements for the three lectures to be delivered.
The first lecture was given at LSE, and I am grateful to Lord
Justice Sedley for chairing the event so well. The second lecture
was delivered at the University of Durham where Professor
Helen Fenwick was a generous and thoughtful chair. My third
and final presentation was held at Queen's University, Belfast:
I am very grateful to Professor Colin Harvey for chairing that
lecture and to Professor Norma Dawson for looking after me
so well during my stay in Belfast. I was received immensely
hospitably at each of the three venues for the lectures, and I
want here to thank in particular the law departments at each
University and also the Centre for the Study of Human Rights
at LSE for having done so much to make each of the three lectures into such enjoyable events. The chair of the Hamlyn
Trustees Professor Kim Economides has been a tremendous
support to me throughout the past year. I cannot praise
enough his dedication to the whole Hamlyn idea, his determination that the lectures should be a success and his extremely
kind and sensitive handling of this particular lecturer throughout the whole and sometimes (for the lecturer fraught) process
of translating some random initial thoughts via three lectures
into book form. A highlight of my association with this year's
lectures has been the opportunity it has given me to publish

with Cambridge University Press for the first time, the press of the University in which I obtained my graduate degrees and where I spent many very happy years as a teacher of law. The embodiment of the Press for Hamlyn purposes has been Finola O'Sullivan and it gives me great pleasure to acknowledge my debt to her; it is her combination of solidarity with the author (when it is craved), intellectual acumen (when it is needed) and firmness (when it is warranted) that makes her such a pleasure to work with.

These lectures are the product of many years of discussion and conversation in many different classes at both King's College London and (more recently) LSE. I want to thank all the students I have taught over so many years for the many thoughts and ideas that they have given me: I am lucky enough to be able to say that I enjoy teaching as much now as when I gave my first supervision in constitutional law at Wolfson College Cambridge in 1982. I would also like to thank the Rausing Trust, and in particular Sigrid Rausing, for their generosity in funding the Rausing Directorship of the Centre for the Study of Human Rights at LSE. This has been a wonderful position from which to be able to write and think about human rights. It has also been a terrific place to work, for which I am grateful to the Centre manager Joy Whyte in particular but also to the whole team at the Centre – the atmosphere in the place makes my visits to work seem more like pleasure than business.

In thinking through the lectures last summer and then in writing them up for this book, I have had the benefit of comments and suggestions from a number of people. Several of those who attended the lectures either spoke to me at the time or wrote to me subsequently, and I am grateful to them all. Special thanks go to Jon Benjamin, Brian Bix, Matt Cavanagh, Christine Chinkin, Stan Cohen, Hugh Collins, Oliver Davies, Abigail Eshel, Jones Hanvey S.J., Carol Harlow, Reuben Hasson, Francesca Klug, Peter Leyland, Martin Loughlin, Niki Lacey, Virginia Mantevelou, Claire Moon, John Phillips, Gerard Quinn, Rick Rawlings, Richard Rorty, Nick Russell, Margot Salomon, Colin Scott, Stephen Sedley, Rabinder Singh, Adam Tomkins and Diane Wales. I would like to dedicate this book to my two wonderful children, Eliza and Owen, who are not only a couple of very lovable individuals but are also great fun to be with.

Conor Gearty
London
February 2006

1

Introduction

This book is about one of the great civilising achievements of the modern era. It traces the rise of human rights and explains why it is that their protection is now thought to be so important in so many walks of life, and across so many different continents and cultures. The chapters that follow cover the subject from its various angles, the legal, the political, the international, the philosophical and so on: if a concise account of human rights is what is desired, then these pages aim to deliver. But there is something else going on here as well, revealed by my title, 'Can Human Rights Survive?' This is not a book that celebrates the past while planning confidently for the future: there is no certainty of a happy ending. The idea of human rights is a fine one, and it has clearly been successful, but that does not mean that it is guaranteed to be so in perpetuity. A perspective on the world that is prospering today does not inevitably thrive tomorrow. The subject faces serious challenges. Unless these are squarely confronted and seen off, there is a risk that the idea will be destroyed for ever, or at best subverted out of all present recognition. In what follows I detail what these challenges to human rights are and I also provide a strategy for how I say we can rise above them. The book, therefore, is not only a retelling of the human rights story but is two other things as well: a warning against complacency and an intellectual manifesto for a successful human rights future.

The chapters that follow are also partly autobiographical, an exercise in a kind of old-style apologetics. I know firsthand of the seriousness of the threats posed by opponents of human rights because I used to be one of them myself. I had – and still have – a high regard for the arguments of the sceptics. My journey to and from human rights atheism began when I started teaching law in Britain in the early 1980s. Before then, educated in Ireland, I was an enthusiast for human rights of an entirely orthodox sort: bills of rights were great; judges even better; majoritarian democracy stinks; and so on. I took with gusto to the conversion of Britain to my human-rights-oriented point of view, one that I was delighted to find shared by almost all the public lawyers I met. Only the Westminster politicians took a different view, unreasonably clinging (as I saw it at the time) to the life-raft of parliamentary sovereignty, like a bunch of castaways from true, rights-based civilisation. Then I began to notice the cases that were flowing from the courts, a trickle at first but soon afterwards a flood: on the miners' strike, on *Spycatcher*, on Northern Ireland, above all on the various miscarriages of justice that came to dominate the legal scene in the 1980s and early 1990s.[1] I had to teach all these dreadful, coercive decisions while saying *at the same time* that the judges should be relied upon to defend freedom and human rights via a new constitutional settlement. It was absurd: manifestly these were not men (and they were practically all men) who could be relied upon to do this job. But they were the only judges we had and they were not likely to change anytime soon.

---

[1] For a fairly full account see K.D. Ewing and C.A. Gearty, *Freedom under Thatcher. Civil Liberties in Modern Britain* (Oxford University Press, Oxford, 1990).

Further misgivings rushed into the breach in my beliefs opened up by the judges' bad behaviour, accelerating my drift to human rights hostility. Judges were bad everywhere, not just in Britain. They had been even worse in the past – there had never been a golden age of judicial good conduct; this was just a liberal myth.[2] Even seemingly progressive human rights cases, like the US decision permitting abortion *Roe v Wade*,[3] were bad decisions when you looked more closely at them, causing more harm in the long tem than the good they did in individual cases. And what was so awful about democracy anyway? It was a simple idea, the government of a community by its representatives: only those who wanted to subvert it fuzzed it up with pompous talk of inalienable rights and spurious fear-mongering about the 'tyranny of the majority'. To cap it all, there were no such things as human rights: they were a mere trick of the language, without any foundational base in truth or empirical reality. When I applied for my current job, as Rausing Director of the Centre for the Study of Human Rights at LSE, the first question at interview was why, given I was such a well-known opponent of human rights, I had bothered to apply.

The answer I gave then is the bridge across which I have ever since been shuffling the intellectual material with which I have reconstructed my belief in human rights, recovering my enthusiasm for the subject, while at the same time not reneging on the perspective that had fuelled my earlier

---

[2] For the best development of this point that I have read see K.D. Ewing, 'The Bill of Rights Debate: Democracy or Juristocracy in Britain', in K.D. Ewing, C.A. Gearty, and B.A. Hepple (eds.), *Human Rights and Labour Law* (Mansell, London, 1994).   [3] 410 US 113 (1973).

scepticism. Bills of rights, written constitutions, judicial decisions on rights and so on are not, I said, the whole of the
human rights story; they are merely means to an end. That end
is the proper achievement of human rights. If these methods
of securing this end fail then they should be condemned.
Judicially-enforced bills of rights do fail. It followed that to
deplore such defective means was to be more of a human rights
enthusiast than those who promoted their mere existence as
sufficient in itself to warrant celebration. And as to the nature
of these human rights goals to which all else was subject? Here
the answer became and still is rather general. 'Human rights'
is the phrase that comes to mind when we want to capture in
words a particular view of the world that we share with others
and that we aspire to share with still greater numbers of
people. That view is one rooted in the simple insight that each
of us counts, that we are each equally worthy of esteem. This
esteem is not on account of what we do, or how we look, or
how bright we are, or what colour we are, or where we come
from, or our ethnic group: it is simply on account of the fact
that we are.

To esteem someone is not necessarily to like that
person, still less to have to admire or approve of him or her. All
these states of mind suggest attributes in the other that warrant
or justify such feelings on our part. Esteem does none of those
things; it involves no one in any kind of talent or beauty
contest. There is no entry fee or preliminary judgment day.
What esteem requires of us is that we see individuals as exactly
that, as first and foremost particular persons, just like us.
Human rights is in this sense a visibility project: its driving
focus is to get us to see the people around us, particularly those

whom we might otherwise (only slightly metaphorically speaking) not see at all, or those whom we would try to ignore if we did catch a glimpse of them. It follows that, at its core, human rights is a subject that is concerned with the outsider, with the marginalised, and with the powerless – these are the various individuals and groups of individuals who in any given culture or time are most likely to be invisible to those around them, who are most liable to find themselves pushed beyond the periphery of a community's field of vision, or who are viewed as non- or sub-human if they are seen. It is these people who need human rights protection the most.

This right of each individual to be treated with as much esteem as any other unfolds into two further categories of entitlements, each derived from this insight about esteem but carrying the concept closer to practical realisation in our daily lives. The first emphasises what the idea of human rights demands should *not* be done, the second speaks in more positive terms about what *ought* to be striven for. Turning to the first of these, it is clear that closest of all to our macro-principle of esteem is the idea of equality which in this context manifests itself as a prohibition on unjustifiable discrimination: the insistence that none of us should find ourselves treated disadvantageously solely on account of some characteristic – our colour, our ethnicity, our gender for example – which is not clearly germane to the task at hand or to the service we desire to receive. Human rights also insists that none of us should be used as mere instruments of another, reduced to a means deployed by another for his or her ends. We each of us have a right to life and also a right not to be treated cruelly, by being tortured or subjected to inhuman or degrading treatment. We have a similarly

5

absolute right not to be reduced to slavery or otherwise forced into servitude at the command of another. These various rights follow from the duty imposed on all of us not to reduce our fellow individuals to non-human packages to do with what we will. Where their breach occurs in a discriminatory way we have the most horrific human rights abuse of all, genocide.

This negative side of human rights, the version of the subject that is all about bad news, human horrors and how to prevent them, is an important strand to our subject, but it is not the only one. It is clear both from the way in which we use the term and from the breadth, range and aspirations of the international human rights movement that there is more to the phrase than this bleak prospectus. This is where our second category comes into play. Human rights has an upbeat dimension as well, one that stresses positive human potentialities rather than our dismally ineradicable inclination to harm each other. This strand speaks to the right that each of us has in view of our humanity to make the best of our capacities, to do well, to lead lives that close to their end we will be able to look back upon and call successful. Human flourishing has been brought by linguistic usage and the actions of activist civil society well within the rubric of the term human rights. This part of our subject speaks to our right to thrive, not only as individuals but also through those associations and connections – with family, community, culture, national identity and so on – by which our humanity is further enriched. This is the part of the human rights story that celebrates difference and diversity. It recognises that we do not all have to follow the same pathways to this kind of success. So whereas the universals in the first branch of our subject are clear for all to see – do not discriminate unjustly;

do not use others solely as instruments of your own will – the generalisations here are broader, less prescriptive, more emancipatory – give everybody a chance; open up opportunities for all; empower people to do the best they can.

If all this sounds rather broad, then it is a breadth that has been increasingly embraced by legal and political communities across the world over the past several decades. I return to this in more detail when I trace the growth of human rights in chapter 2. For now it is enough to note that the Universal Declaration of Human Rights, agreed in 1948, reflects a broad commitment to our subject, one that embraces both of the aspects of it we have just been discussing. That acclaimed document contains not just the expected prohibitions on cruelty but also an agenda of action to improve the lives of the peoples of the world, the kinds of things we might come up if we were designing Nirvana from scratch. There are prohibitions on torture, on cruel, inhuman and degrading treatment, and an absolute ban on slavery, servitude and the slave trade. But there are also guarantees of the good life, 'the economic, social and cultural rights' that are 'indispensable for [a person's] dignity and the free development of his [or her] personality'.[4] The same is true of the various other international agreements that have followed that declaration, in particular the Covenants on Civil and Political Rights and on Economic, Social and Cultural Rights, both agreed in 1966. Here the rights set out in the Universal Declaration are fleshed out and given a degree of international enforceability. Regional bills of rights (such as the European Convention on Human Rights) provide

---

[4] Article 22.

a similar kind of service for groups of states, albeit usually with a stronger enforcement arm. Most embedded of all are the domestic bills of rights now to be found scattered around the globe, some with very wide socio-economic reach, others with civil and political priorities but all taking the subject far further than the prohibition of cruelty and of unjustifiable discrimination. The South African bill of rights is the strongest example of this, but there are many others as well. We probe into these domestic human rights instruments in greater detail in chapter 3.

Matching this legal success has been the growing ascendancy of this broad version of human rights in the political sphere. This also bears closer examination later, in chapter 2, but what has been increasingly evident in recent years has been an increased sense of the need to articulate political goals in rights terms. This began with the post-World War II desire to reshape the concept of democracy to include rather than undermine the idea of rights. Since the end of the Cold War, human rights as a subject of political discourse has really taken off, with more and more of the peoples of the world embracing this language as a way of organising political debate and of informing their relations with the world. The category of human rights has increasingly appeared to be an open one, capable of being filled with meaning by those anxious to use it to improve the lot of their fellow beings, of achieving greater success for our species, and thereby handing on to the next generation a better set of prospects than they themselves have inherited. So all-embracing has been the language of human rights of late that it has seemed at times impossible to articulate a vision of the future without lapsing into its vernacular.

8

Where once we had ideas like 'socialism', 'social justice' and 'fairness', nowadays increasingly 'human rights' is being called upon to do all the moral work.

Here though is the beginning of the rub. True, this recent triumph of human rights idea suggests that it should be foolhardy or just besides the point to question its continued success. Part of me agrees: the phrase is doing broadly speaking good work, and surely it would be better now to suppress all those residual qualms that I might still have from my hostile past and join whole-heartedly in the celebration? But this is to do the subject what would ultimately be a disservice, for it is exactly at moments of apparently greatest triumph like these that dangers can be found lurking in the margins, perils which, if left unnoticed, could well soon spread and damage the whole. This is where the old sceptic returns, keen to desta- bilise – but not in order to destroy this time, rather with the purpose of re-securing and rebuilding for the future. Three areas of the subject as it has developed in recent years are a cause of particular concern, and these have stimulated the crises which I identify and tackle in the three chapters that are at the core of this book.

First there is the crisis of authority. Why is it that human rights has moved onto so much ethical territory, to the exclusion of other moral notions that have done useful work in their day? It suggests a subject with a strong set of founda- tions underpinning this moral colonialism, and indeed the idea of human rights has long been wedded to notions of truth and moral obligation. Its supporters have always needed to be able to answer convincingly the sort of questions that sceptics ask: 'where do these human rights you insist on come from?';

'how do we know we have these human rights?'; 'who tells us what the content of human rights is?'; crudest of all, 'why should I care about my fellow humans, if they are not related to me or even from my community? – their suffering or failure to flourish is no concern of mine'. In the old days the response used to be fairly simple. The human rights advocate being questioned in this way could choose between two answers depending on which suited the sceptical questioner more. Either 'Your God insists that you act towards others in this way, because these other people, these strangers, are special, made by your God and therefore have a right to your esteem'; or (for the more rationally inclined) 'When you work through in your mind what it involves to be human, you will see that it makes sense to develop the kind of set of moral obligations that we are calling human rights.' To anxieties about how to spot what the content of these human rights actually was, and therefore how to act in a practical way, the answer that used to work was simply to say that it was necessary to consult the moral boss, either the priest or the professor depending on which of the first alternates to the fundamental question had proved satisfactory.

Now it will be entirely clear that this sort of thing doesn't work anymore, or at least does not do so effectively in twenty-first century developed society, precisely the environment in which the idea of human rights has risen to such prominence. In such places, neither religion nor reason has the hold that each once had. The philosophical movement since the end of the nineteenth century has been away from truth and external, observable realities, and towards doubt, indeterminacy and contingency. The talk has all been of talk – the importance of words and language usage – and of agreement about meaning: not what the words actually mean but what we collectively say they mean, which it is now said is the very best we can hope for in this age of uncertainty. Despite its legal and political success, the idea of 'human rights' has been looking more and more like an awkward and ill-fitting old relative at the philosophical house parties of recent years, standing in the corner muttering about reality and 'a sense of moral obligation' while all about the young thinkers are jiving away grabbing what truth they can from the wordplay swirling about. So we have a paradox: the idea of human rights has been reaching dizzying heights in the worlds of politics and law whilst its philosophical base has been increasingly called into question, challenged as to its very existence in ways that would have been unthinkable in previous epochs, when the term was not nearly so powerful or so successful. This mismatch cannot go on indefinitely: the subject of human rights needs a better answer to the question of the basis of its authority than it seems currently able to provide, and if it fails to deliver such a response then its medium to long term future cannot be assured. In chapter 2 I seek to make the whole human rights building altogether more secure, or at least as secure as it can be in these insecure times.

The crises in chapters 3 and 4 grow out of the philosophical vacuum that is the subject of chapter 2. Each reflects what can happen to a term which achieves popularity without clarity as to its meaning. The 'crisis of legalism' discussed in chapter 3 explores the various problems that come with the successful embedding of the term 'human rights' in our legal discourse. It is at one level a wonderful thing for any idea to be made part of the law, and even more marvellous for it to be included in a country's fundamental code such as its constitution or its basic bill of rights. Human rights often achieve the latter state of supreme legal authority, as high a summit as it is possible for any mere notion to aspire to within the discourse of law. But if we recall that our subject is primarily about empowering the voiceless and the marginalised and then remind ourselves that law is not generally seen as a radical or even a progressive tool – quite the reverse in fact – when we do this, we are left with the problem of *authentic* enforcement. What I mean by this is that we have to recognise that we are relying on a largely speaking conservative force – the law, the judges, the legal profession – to carry our radical project through to completion. But which great social movement has ever before put the lawyers in its front-line? What kind of a war-strategy is it to entrust our greatest emancipatory tasks to judges, a sub-category of precisely the kind of well-off, already empowered person who ought to be terrified by the prospect of true human rights? In this chapter we ask how human rights can be carried forward into law, as carried forward they must be, without being drained of all their energy and zest in the process. In particular, we consider how they can be kept part of the maelstrom of the politics that has given rise to them and not quarantined in the reactionary but omnipotent realms of the law. Bridging the gap that has opened up between the two ways in which law and politics treat human rights is the key to the survival of our subject in the face of the particular challenge considered in chapter 3.

Chapter 4, 'the crisis of national security', looks at the price of success not in the legal but in a particular and important political field. When human rights amounted to not much more that a tiny, faraway dot on our democratic radar they tended to be ignored by our political leadership, or turned into a tool of international relations if they were spotted at all. That changed with the success of the term in the post-Cold War era. When everybody started clambering aboard the human rights wagon, government leaders started to do so as well. In the old days, pre-1989, you could tell how undemocratic a country was by how loudly it proclaimed itself to be a democracy in its national description. Things are not quite as bad as this with human rights, but if we are not careful they will get there. Human rights protection is such an apparently self-evident good, so clearly the right thing to do, that leaders with ulterior motives have been unable to resist deploying the term as a basis for action. In the domestic sphere we have seen increasingly illiberal and restrictive terrorism laws being passed around the world, and these have been invariably presented not as in conflict with but rather as in accord with the prevailing human rights norms: either the declared emergency is a human-rights-consistent suspension of human rights or the attack on freedom under examination turns out on closer scrutiny not to be an attack at all, to be in fact compatible with human rights because 'necessary in a democratic society' or for some other such exculpatory but human-rights-based reason. Thus does the idea of human rights get punished for its success by being taken over and turned into a force for the legitimisation of cruelty and oppression.

As I say this has not happened yet to a very great extent, but unless we pay close attention to the foundations of our subject and attend to its health as critical friends rather than bland cheerleaders, there is every possibility that it might do so. The point has a foreign policy dimension as well. The rallying power of the term human rights has proved itself very useful in those reasonably functioning democracies where the consent of the governed is more or less required for large-scale government decisions but where military action abroad has become increasingly unpopular as a tool for the promotion of a nation's interests overseas. In this final substantive chapter we also look at the damage done to the emancipatory power of human rights, and to its capacity to speak for the powerless and the disenfranchised, by its being deployed as a rationale for military action. Whatever the short-term benefits of such usage, the damaging long term effect on the integrity of human rights is immense: behind every Kosovo, there is, we are forced glumly to conclude, an Iraq waiting to happen.

The core chapters that follow this introduction provide an agenda for action so far as each of the particular themes with which they deal are concerned. A recurring leit-motif in this book is the idea of human rights as a mask – one of truth in chapter 2, of legality in chapter 3 and of national self-interest in chapter 4. My agenda for action requires us to think about what to do with each of these masks, whether to leave them on, allow them to be cast off if needs be or rejected completely – broadly speaking these are the three suggestions for chapters 2, 3 and 4 respectively. Another running theme is the contrast between the general and the particular. Human rights is by definition concerned with the individual, with ensuring that the vulnerable among us are noticed and then given the solicitous attention each deserves. How can human rights realise this goal on a grand scale? Critics of the subject say that it is ultimately only about the occasional individual act of charity and that it has no coherent political framework for transforming its compassionate instincts into a truly progressive politics. They make the point that the concern demanded by human rights for the particular, for this or that individual, in the end holds back the subject, denies it the capacity for progress enjoyed by more robust and less sentimental philosophies (like utilitarianism and socialism for example). An answer to this powerful critique emerges from the way in which our subject is aligned with truth (in chapter 2) and with democracy (in chapter 3) – and because the point is so important I return to it again in chapter 4 where the dangers of turning human rights into a set of abstract values rather than an ethic with an individual focus are (I hope) laid out for all to see.

In my final chapter, I consider what more needs to be done to consolidate a successful future for human rights. I ask how the idea can be made to work properly to solve emerging problems such as those related to the right to life, to genetic engineering, and the right to die. I ask how human rights activists should relate to other social forces for change such as the environmental and animal rights movements. And I consider which kinds of attitudes should be considered as not capable of being preserved within the human rights tent, large though it is. My aim is to end on an upbeat note, to deliver a prognosis which is optimistic about the future but stern about what the patient must do now to avoid declining health later. Human rights can survive, but their supporters must think harder, run with rather than against democracy, not be afraid of making powerful enemies, and be choosier about what they stand for while willing to build alliances with the forces of justice and fairness wherever they find them.

2

The crisis of authority

How does it *feel* to know what the truth is when you are every-where surrounded by doubt? The feeling itself is undoubtedly marvellous to enjoy; it suffuses the body with a glow of cer-tainty, impelling action where others can muster only cynical inactivity. The emotions say: life is worth living; we have a goal, a purpose: we believers are special. But this superabundance of feeling is watched with dismay by the brain. Truth is its pre-serve after all and it is not so sure: if we are right, then all around are wrong; where are the facts, the data that make us so special, that make sense of and therefore explain and support our joyous certainty? New information keeps pouring into the mind, often threatening to subvert our feelings with fresh ways of describing the world that simply don't fit with our *felt* knowledge. Is the mind to be our praetorian guard, barring contrary thoughts from entering our emotional conscious-ness? Or should it in the name of truth join the sceptics and fight raw feeling with disagreeable news from the world of learning?

Jürgen Habermas has remarked of religious beliefs that they require 'striking cognitive dissonances' since, as he puts it, 'the complex life circumstances in modern pluralistic societies are normatively compatible only with a *strict* universalism in which the same respect is demanded for everybody – be they Catholic, Protestant, Muslim, Jewish, Hindu, or Buddhist, believers or nonbelievers'.[1] But in comparison with believers in human rights, religious followers have it easy. Often they are not from 'modern pluralistic societies' at all and so can feel quite at home without a shadow of Habermas-inspired doubt finding its way into their epistemic consciousness. Even if they are, they have many bulwarks against crisis available to them – the confidence of a way of life that has been around for centuries; the support of a community of believers; the leadership of decisive figures, perhaps even a structure of authority that protects the mind from external challenge; above all confidence in some kind of God or spirit that speaks directly to the situation of his or her followers, both individually and collectively. For some exceptionally lucky believers there is even the bonus of eternal life at some point in the post-future.

By comparison, the human rights believers are lonely and vulnerable. They seek Heaven on earth and for all not just (or even mainly) for themselves or the chosen few. It is firmly within 'the complex life circumstances in modern pluralistic societies' that they must ply their trade. They cannot thrive outside pluralism: to the extent that human rights instincts are to be found in the world of certainty where the religious believers are still at home then it is as a benign branch of whatever the prevailing religion happens to be. But pluralism's shelter for human rights leaks with doubt: in a place where everything is true, nothing can be *really* true. Human rights people are stuck, required without the support of many symbols to practise their beliefs in exactly those places – developed

[1] G. Borradori, *Philosophy in a Time of Terror. Dialogues with Jürgen Habermas and Jacques Derrida* (University of Chicago Press, Chicago and London, 2004) p. 32.

modern societies – where belief in anything is hard enough and belief in something moral apparently rooted in human nature hardest of all. They are the disciples of an idea rather than a sacred text or even a holy (much less a divine) person, and the closest they get to congregational worship is the occasional drinks party after a human rights lecture. (They are usually too polite for the solidarity that comes from public protest.)

If the idea of human rights amounts to, as my colleague Francesca Klug has put it, a set of 'values for a Godless age',[2] then their custodians face a tough task. As I have already observed in Chapter 1, the phrase 'human rights' is a strong one, epistemologically confident, ethically assured, carrying with it a promise to the hearer to cut through the noise of assertion and counter-assertion, of cultural practices and relativist perspectives, and thereby to deliver truth. To work its moral magic, human rights needs to exude this kind of certainty, this old-fashioned clarity. Without it, what else is there to give meaning to the term? Are human rights to be just whatever feels right? Is it enough to assert the importance of esteem or equal treatment or equality of respect as the basis of human rights but then to avoid discussion of where these ideas come from? To echo the sorts of questions I have already asked in chapter 1, why not hurt our neighbour, grab all we can from the passing stranger, walk past the hungry homeless with unmoved heart? How can the idea of human rights provide an answer to these questions without an appeal to truth? The subject is stuck with truth, and non-religious truth at that. Yet 'truth', knowing 'right' from 'wrong', 'moral obligation' and so

---

2 F. Klug, *Values for a Godless Age. The Story of the United Kingdom's New Bill of Rights* (Penguin Books, London, 2000).

on are notions that seem to come from another age, like calling Radio Four the Home Service or the *Guardian* the *Manchester Guardian* – their very deployment seems to date the user.

There is a preliminary objection to the whole thrust of this chapter that I have already touched on briefly in chapter 1. Would it not be better to question less and act more, to avoid reflection on abstract ideas like philosophical foundations and the like but to continue to use the term 'human rights' to do good things in a world in which goodness is in short supply – and where it is a waste of time and effort to spend time trying to explain what goodness actually means? On this view, human rights scholarship is above all activist scholarship and human rights advocates are impressively practical in their approach to the world. It is true that at the moment, the term 'human rights' has ethical cachet. It enjoys moral power. As a short-hand description of how we want to improve the world it works very well. But it is not guaranteed to do this all the time. We are trading on the force that was put into the term by past generations, first those who saw it as a branch of religion and then those (in the modern era) who gave it its secular, rationalist twist. Residues of commitment to both these visions of the world remain in pluralist society, and because of this the idea of 'human rights', half pre-modern/half modern, continues to enjoy a warm reception. But as post-modern uncertainty embeds itself more deeply in our culture, and as our memory of religious and Enlightenment times fades, so our commitment to this benign relic of both can be expected to begin to recede.

Without a reworking of what the term 'human rights'

means today, designed to give it contemporary intellectual confidence, some theoretical zest, then the time might come when firing the human rights argument will be greeted neither with warmth nor dismay but rather with blank indifference, or (which is worse) mute incomprehension: whatever can that term mean? Is it not of merely historical interest these days, part of what we used to be rather than what we have become? Or even worse the term might be known but have taken a different shape: 'oh, human rights are fine but of course they are not for everybody, just us'. The great utilitarian philosopher Jeremy Bentham famously condemned natural rights as 'nonsense upon stilts'.[3] He meant by this that they were an absurdity so extreme that they required to be raised high above the rest of the mere nonsense that surrounded them. But viewed another way, stilts are at least a support of sorts, a foundation for something – albeit a flimsy one. Perhaps a modern day, post-modern Bentham would deride our subject as 'nonsense without stilts'. To survive, our subject must refute this critique.

The elusive 'golden age'

What would certainly infuriate a latter-day Bentham is how this 'nonsense without stilts' seems to bloom. Like some kind of mysterious plant that can thrive only when not rooted firmly in the soil, human rights as an idea defies its apparent philosophical shallowness and goes from strength to strength in both the political and legal arenas. The subject has however

---

[3] See J. Waldron (ed.), 'Nonsense upon Stilts': Bentham, Burke and Marx on the Rights of Man (Metheun Books, London, 1987), p. 53.

never been lucky in its intellectual apologists; its early heroes are not good at transcending their particular moment and speaking clearly to us today. The Greeks knew all about justice, natural justice, fairness and the like but did not have the words to describe the notion of a subjective right, of a set of entitlements invested in a person on simple account of their humanity. The Roman Church embraced the concept of natural law with enthusiasm and saw in it a variety of propositions that could be taken to be indelibly true, but in its initial form and for centuries afterwards this notion of objective right did not stray into subjective territory: a right was in the air, not in the bodies walking the earth beneath. With its emphasis on individuality, the Protestant reformation completed the process. When subjective right did emerge, its originally very Christian basis makes it an uncertain ally in our contemporary, highly secular culture. Other faiths and religious systems that were established or flourished around the same time as Christianity had many ideas of duty, fellowship, solidarity and so on, but it would be stretching things too far to say that they had any kind of refined concept of a set of what we understand today to be individually-based human rights.[4]

---

[4] M.R. Ishay, *The Human Rights Reader* (Routledge, New York, 1997), pp. 1–72 has some very useful documents from the various religious traditions. Especially good on faith-based approaches to human rights is J. Mahoney, *The Challenge of Human Rights* (Blackwell Publishing, Oxford, 2006 [in press]). One writer whose contribution to the development of a modern discourse of human rights is hugely underestimated is Hugo Grotius: see M.R. Ishay, *The History of Human Rights* (University of California Press, Berkeley, California, 2004), pp. 99–101 and Ishay, *The Human Rights Reader* pp. 73–84 (extracts from Grotius's *On Laws of War and Peace* (1625)).

All this large-scale missing of the mark by classical and medieval thinkers meant that the field was clear for three fantasists of human nature to seize an initiative which has never been quite surrendered ever since: Hobbes, Locke and Rousseau. It is certainly the case that the language of human rights came to the fore in the seventeenth and eighteenth centuries. But the foundations put down are not of the kind that we can recover and put to work today. The English tradition epitomised by Hobbes and Locke sees the individual as the bearer of pre-political rights with government a necessary but unpleasant antidote to anarchy. Rousseau saw things exactly the other way round: freedom needed to be achieved rather than surrendered – it flowed out of rather than preceded the authority of the general will of the people, expressed through law. Each of these versions of human nature went on to underpin violent revolution, in England in 1688 and in France and what became the United States a century later, and there is nothing like a successful revolution to embed an idea in the collective mind of a culture. But the 'human rights' bit of Locke soon lost out to its power-to-government corollary (what today we call the sovereignty of parliament), albeit laced with a liberal individualism that is grumpy about official power and still nostalgic for its pre-political golden age. Rousseau's unfortunate ramble about forcing people to be free was dubious even when it was written and has not been improved by the horrors that have since been done in the name of compulsory freedom. America's sweeping declaration of independence quickly plummeted via a much narrower constitutional bill of rights into a provincial legalism from which the culture has yet to emerge: I will talk a little about this disastrous legalisation of American rights in chapter 3. As for the French Declaration of the Rights of Man and of the Citizen, it was to go down in a hail of fire not only at Waterloo but also (speaking metaphorically) before the scorching assaults of those influential nineteenth-century thinkers who were to dominate their respective fields for over 100 years: Bentham, Burke and Marx.

I should take a moment to identify why the nineteenth-century critique of our subject was so effective: these writers' remarks still need to be addressed if the gap between, on the one hand, the current political and legal success of human rights and, on the other, its contemporary philosophical uncertainty is to be successfully closed. [5] Jeremy Bentham's main point about human rights was to stress that they got in the way of that proper commitment to human happiness which should be the goal of all our endeavours. His focus on ends rather than means – reflected in the philosophy of utilitarianism with which he will be forever associated – is subversive of human rights, and I will later in this chapter return to it, to see whether the version of human rights I develop here can answer its modern day utilitarian critics better than could the rights' advocates of Bentham's age. Edmund Burke's emphasis on history rather than on reason made him mistrust the grandiloquent articulacy of the rights-language of his day with its excessive emphasis on artificial, ahistorical and pre-political worlds. Focusing on substance rather than outward forms, Karl Marx castigated human rights as a vehicle for individual

---

[5] Waldron, '*Nonsense upon Stilts*', n. 3 above, is the best and most accessible place to find them. Waldron's critique in the book is also well worth reading.

aggrandisement and enrichment of the privileged classes. To work effectively, what I have to say here about human rights will need to be able to cope with these critics as well. I think this task is achievable. The positions of Bentham, Burke and Marx are reasonably well-known and have long been chewed over by human rights defenders. They can be answered by presenting a defence of the authority of human rights along the lines that I will be developing later in this chapter.

The rise and rise of human rights

After being seen off by the combined antagonism of these three intellectual giants of the modern age, the idea of human rights in the nineteenth century went into a decline that would have surprised those who had witnessed its apparently irresistible rise the century before. True there were great strides made towards the abolition of slavery, and moral recoil at the savagery of mid-nineteenth-century conflict did lead to the development of what was eventually to grow into an extensive code of humanitarian law. But human rights as such, as a big idea informing the way the world thought of itself, was in this period largely superseded by the rise of first the democratic and then the socialist ideal: these were the goals towards which the energies of the progressive forces of the time were directed. The First World War provided a strong push towards both, creating the conditions for Bolshevik revolution in Russia and producing at its conclusion a fresh commitment to democratic nation-building among the victorious powers. By 1930, there seemed no reason to suppose that there would be any change in this state of affairs: the end of empire had embedded democracy as

25

the common sense of a large part of the developed world, while the construction of Stalin's Union of Soviet Republics now seemed also to presage an alternative, equally robust, socialist future. The turning point for human rights came at exactly this apparent pinnacle of success for democracy and socialism. The next ten years were a nightmare of brutality, show trials and mass killings and at their end came total war, concentration camps and the Holocaust. By 1945 much of the world was ready for a new language, one that was idealistic whilst being neither merely democratic nor prescriptively socialist. Flailing around for words both to describe why what had happened in the war just past was so bad, and at the same time striving also to delineate a future that could be shown to have been worth fighting for, the narrators of the age found what they wanted in the discarded rhetoric of the Enlightenment.

The Universal Declaration of Human Rights in 1948 marked the foundation of the new human rights era, and its breadth – encompassing both social and economic as well as civil and political rights – made it a document to which all sides in the fast-emerging Cold War felt able to commit themselves. Progress was still slow. As efforts intensified to translate the sentiments of the Universal Declaration into tangible advances, so the term 'human rights' became increasingly caught up in the Soviet/American quarrel. Washington condemned Moscow's denial of civil and political freedoms while glossing over the inequalities that littered its own back yard. For its part, the Soviet commitment to 'human rights' as that term was understood in the West was entirely tactical: the Eastern bloc still saw human rights in the way that Marx had seen them, as highly individualistic and as a support for –

rather than subversive of – the power of capital. It was the political reforms of the Gorbachev era in the 1980s that exposed the Soviet Union's true position and catastrophically undermined the Stalinist brand of socialism that under-pinned both that regime and those of its various satellites. The changes came with remarkable speed, in 1989. With the end of the Cold War and the consequent failure of socialism to maintain (for the time being at least) an ideological chal-lenge to capitalism, the phrase 'human rights' has been able for the first time to step fully onto the centre-stage that the Universal Declaration had erected for it. Socialists, trade unionists and radicals have found themselves joining liberals and Christian democrats in the human rights camp. Even David Cameron's newly-branded Conservative Party in Britain seems to want to climb aboard a bandwagon that looks as though it is here to stay.

A further impetus behind the subject's rise has been the surge in globalisation that has been the most noteworthy development in the post-Cold War world. Though undoubt-edly a good thing in many ways, the debilitating side-effects of globalisation have been many – among others: the collapse in a large number of society's support structures; the apparent power of capital to claw back social concessions that had been made in previous more socialist eras; an increase in the gap between rich and poor; and the reduction in personal and family security. In such a context, and without the ballast of socialist or religious certainty, the idea of human rights has sought, with some success, to hold back the tide of the market and of unmediated self-interest. Human rights feeds what has been well described as the 'genuine hunger in people, a post-material quest for anchors of meaning'[6] that is evident in this global age, a support moreover that promises to be more effective than the past anchors of religion and reason. Indeed, at times recently it has seemed that it has only been this barely rooted plant that has lain between us and capitalist anarchy.

Darwin, thought and truth

The failure of Hobbes, Locke and Rousseau to speak to us convincingly today remains, however. So too does the fact that human rights has no 'golden age' from the past on whch to draw for contemporary moral sustenance. The task of this chapter should now be clear. If human rights are to survive, it is imperative to translate the political and legal success of the idea into the philosophical arena, to construct non-nonsensical foundations for human rights, support systems that defend the idea not by the simple invocation of past glories but in terms that ring true today, that run with rather than against the grain of contemporary assumptions about what it means to be right and wrong. Neither the religious nor the rational defenders of human rights are as persuasive as they used to be and we have already encountered the strength of the criticism levelled by that triad of nineteenth-century thinkers, Bentham, Burke and Marx. But great though their scepticism was, I do not see these three well-known figures as the main obstacles to the

---

[6] The phrase is that of Michael Paul Gallagher, 'Struggle and Conversion' *The Tablet* 10 September 2005, p. 10. However the author believes, rightly, that this hunger provides an opportunity for the 'return of religion': he does not deal with the possibility of human rights as a kind of secular faith, or as providing a better anchor which is what I am suggesting here.

contemporary success of coherent human rights thinking, or the chief reason why uncertainty has crowded in over what were once the very clear foundations of our subject. As I have alread said, I think their criticisms can be met.

While these opponents may have weakened the human rights fighter in the ring, it is another nineteenth-century figure altogether who delivered the near knock-out blow, one that has made a philosophical recovery to match recent political and legal success so difficult. I am thinking of Charles Darwin. I appreciate that Darwin may seem an eccentric figure upon whom to alight at this juncture: he was hardly a human rights sceptic, much less a philosopher of any sort, and his fame does not obviously fit our narrative. But human rights needs to confront the challenge of Darwin and what has followed from Darwin; in its buckling before his model of the world lie the seeds of the idea's second coming. I see Darwin as finishing off for good the Enlightenment version of our subject, but at the same time making possible its effective reconstruction for our post post-modern, global age. So he is central to this chapter and to the book as a whole. Indeed I would go so far to say that whether or not human rights can survive largely depends on how we make sense of the breakthroughs that Darwin achieved. First the buckling of our subject before him; later the second coming.

To understand Darwin's impact we need to remind ourselves of a logical truth about human rights. In its modern form it is a subject that depends above all on thought. It is not something that emerges from our bodies as a feeling or an emotion, something like love, hate, anger, or even a sense of unfairness, might be thought to do: the concept of human rights needs brain power to drive it, to explain what it involves and to tell us what, as a result, we *ought* to do. It has more work to do in this regard even than ideas like justice and fairness which come more readily from our gut. Its fertile breeding ground is the mind not the heart. Human rights have thrived in the modern era initiated by Descartes because of the sharp distinction that has been drawn between the mind on the one hand and the body on the other, with a strong emphasis on the overarching importance of the former. Immanuel Kant is the patron saint of these secular celebrators of brain power, and it is no surprise to find that he is also very much the modern Godfather of human rights. But it was Blaise Pascal who perhaps best summed up this perspective when he famously claimed that 'Thought constitutes the very essence of humanity' and went on: 'The human being is just a reed, the weakest thing in nature but it is a thinking reed . . . So our whole dignity consists in thought. That is what we should rely on . . . So let us work at thinking well: that is the basis of morality.'[7] Note the reference to human dignity here – the notion believed by many to be what human rights is all about. And on this world view it is through careful thinking that we work out what to do to foster dignity, and when we have done that human rights are merely a fairly straightforward next step in the argument: the entitlements enjoyed by other persons that flow from what our mind tells us is our moral obligation towards them.

This prioritisation of the mind, so essential to the construction of the idea of human rights, had the handy

---

[7] B. Pascal, *Pascal's Pensées* (Everyman Library, London, 1956), p. 97 quoted in Mahoney, n. 4 above, ms p. 164.

consequence of affirming the uniqueness of humankind, something that these great thinkers were very keen to do.[8] We have minds as well as bodies, none of the other breathing things with which we share the planet have both: whether these minds are God-given or flow from some other source matters less than the fact that they demonstrate our inimitability. This special-ness had not gone unchallenged in the past: David Hume for example had called reason 'the slave of the passions'. But it was Darwin whose breakthroughs on evolution rendered the mind/body distinction impossible to maintain and made the position of human rights so precarious. He 'made it plausible to treat human mental capacities as evolved functions of natural organisms, arising from simpler forms of animal behaviour as a result of their survival-promoting tendencies.'[9] Darwin took our minds out of some unique spiritual ether and put them firmly in our bodies, for how could 'a ghostly mind be linked to the material mind through the bodily machine that it somehow haunts?'[10]

After Darwin it became clear that we are part of our habitat, 'clever animals' as Nietzsche said, differing from the rest only in our greater capacity to redescribe and therefore recreate

[8] Just as it pleased them (hugely) that what they happened to be exceptionally good at (thinking, as opposed to dancing or making love, or sport) was in fact the greatest of all human skills. But is there not a whiff here of special pleading? Might lovers and singers and athletes not feel the same about their skills, but without having the time, ability or motivation to bother to argue the point with dedicated mind-professionals?

[9] T.C. Grey, 'Holmes and Legal Pragmatism' 41 *Stanford Law Review* (1988–89) 787, at p. 796.   [10] *Ibid.* p. 797.

ourselves.[11] Truth could no longer be found by examining the contents of our unique, ethereal minds and reporting back our discoveries like some intrepid internal explorer. There was nothing to report because there was nothing to find and there was nothing to find because there was nothing there, nothing that is apart from the bits and pieces of the organism, all material, into which we had over multiples of generations slowly but surely evolved. The 'humanity is unique' school fought back for a while by leaping upon language as evidence of our specialness: 'We speak, the rest don't,' they cried in desperate triumph. But the point soon fell before the power of the earlier attack. Language was not a medium taking a message from the body out or the world in; it was not an errand-boy from some truth-king lurking eerily in the heavens, in nature or the soul. It was a sub-set of communication, a highly specialised form it was true, but a sub-set nevertheless of something that all animals did, at some basic level or other. What truth there was in language was not foundational in the old sense, but was rather intrinsic to itself: 'truth is a property of sentences, since sentences are dependant for their existence upon vocabularies, and since vocabularies are made by human beings, so are truths.'[12]

The importance of thinking, on which as I have suggested human rights so much depends, has therefore suffered

[11] R. Rorty, *Philosophy and Social Hope* (Penguin Books, London, 1999) pp. 74–75 explores this point as does his Oxford Amnesty lecture from 1993: 'Human Rights, Rationality and Sentimentality', in S. Shute and S. Hurley (eds.), *On Human Rights* (Basic Books, New York, 1993), pp. 111–34.

[12] R. Rorty, *Contingency, Irony, and Solidarity* (Cambridge University Press, Cambridge, 1989) p. 21.

a double-blow which has brought it plummeting from its previously undisputed throne. First we now know that there is no special bit of us, a soul or a mind, exploring what truth is that can then report back its findings and tell us what it is right to do. Second when we think about thinking we look now at our thoughts not as things-beyond-words reported to us by words but rather as indelibly tied up with, made real by, the words themselves. This makes the thought a part of language which is in turn a part of communication. What matters is not what is said but what is understood. Thinking has taken a practical turn. As Oliver Wendell Holmes Junior put it, 'Philosophy as a fellow once said to me is only thinking. Thinking is an instrument of adjustment to the conditions of life – but it becomes an end in itself.'[13] What matters is what happens. To Charles Sanders Peirce, thinking 'was no longer to be conceived as something distinct from practice but rather it simply *was* practice, or activity, in its deliberative or reflective aspect'.[14] As Holmes put it with characteristic succinctness: 'Every idea is an incitement. It offers itself for belief and if believed it is acted on'.[15]

Rhetoric replacing reality

I need now to link this necessarily abstract discussion to human rights. The thrust of what I have been saying is that, first, the idea of human rights depends on thought, and second, that thinking has no existence independent of the words that

[13] Grey, 'Holmes and Legal Pragmatism', p. 853.   [14] *Ibid.* p. 803.
[15] *Gitlow v New York* 268 US 652 (1925) at p. 673 (Holmes J).

articulate sentiments that would otherwise (speaking fig-
uratively) remain lost in the mind. Third, it follows that thinking to be action involving others needs talk or at least
communication, and this in turn requires agreement on
meaning. To say that an organism is a language user 'is just to
say that pairing off the marks and noises it makes with those we
make will prove a useful tactic in predicting and controlling its
future behaviour'.[16] To work in this way, speaker and listener
need to converge on passing theories from utterance to utterance.[17] But if the only truth we can know for sure (a tautology
I know) is our contingent agreement on what certain sounds we
call words mean, where does this leave human rights, a phrase
that seems to tie itself firmly to a very different kind of truth?
The basic approach of human rights foundationalists would
seem to have been left completely behind by this emphasis on
contingency and language. In fact today's defenders of human-
rights-as-universal-truth have been subtler than this, have not
allowed themselves to be boxed-in in this way. On the contrary
they have been craftily moulding their approach to suit the
times – more than perhaps they are sometimes willing to admit.

Even Kant saw conscience as an inner voice, in other
words a kind of private dialogue. Modern attempts at foundationalist thinking in human rights – at saying why human
rights are in fact true – have taken on a strong rhetorical
colour in recent years: increasingly they are exercises in persuasion rather than revelation: 'you have got to believe this'

---

[16] Rorty *Contingency, Irony, and Solidarity* n. 12 above, p. 15.
[17] D. Davidson, 'A Nice Derangement of Epitaphs', quoted in Rorty,
Contingency, Irony, and Solidarity n. 12 above, p. 14.

rather than 'here are my findings'.[18] This explains the theory of human rights as reflecting an overlapping consensus across the world about right behaviour, popularised by John Rawls[19] and (in the human rights field particularly) Jack Donnelly[20] – it must be right because so many people say it. Jürgen Habermas's sophisticated discourse theory leads him to see human rights as facilitative of debate, a way of opening up rather than closing down argument: we look at this in detail in chapter 3 when I consider the inter-relationship between human rights, democracy and law. In his Holdsworth Lecture in November 2005, entitled 'Are human rights universal, and does it matter?', the distinguished intellectual (and judge) Stephen Sedley described most modern-day universalists as no longer claiming 'to be travelling towards a promised land or even a defined goal' but as rather believers in the proposition that 'the process of arguing, urging, campaigning, denouncing, encouraging and asserting advances the world's understanding of human rights and spreads acceptance of them.'[21] I think this is right. The kind of thinking

---

[18] Where this is not the case the theory seems old-fashioned and entirely beside the point: see the criticisms of the work of Alan Gewirth (A. Gewirth, *Human Rights. Essays on Justification and Applications* (University of Chicago Press, Chicago, 1982) in A. MacIntyre, *After Virtue. A Study in Moral Theory* (Duckworth, London, 2nd edn 1985), pp. 66–68 and Mahoney n. 4 above, pp. 151–2.

[19] Especially J. Rawls, 'The Domain of Political and Overlapping Consensus' 64 *New York University Law Review* (1989) no. 2.

[20] J. Donnelly, *Universal Human Rights in Theory and Practice* (Cornell University Press, Ithaca and London, 2nd edn 2003), esp. ch. 3. See also N. Bobbio, *The Age of Rights* (Polity Press, Cambridge, 1996).

[21] The Holdsworth Lecture, University of Birmingham, 25 November 2005, pp. 1–2 (copy with author).

about language that I have just been discussing has been so pervasive that even foundationalists can't help themselves.

Amartya Sen is one of the most impressive of the many contemporary thinkers from a wide variety of intellectual backgrounds who are seeking to solidify the foundations of human rights in the contemporary world. As a Nobel-prize winning economist and former Master of Trinity College Cambridge, Sen's views carry especial weight. On close examination, though, the core of his approach to the subject is rooted in discourse, dialogue and discussion rather than the delivery of objective truth. In an article published in 2004 entitled 'Elements of a Theory of Human Rights',[22] Sen describes 'proclamations of human rights . . . as articulations of ethical demands'. Like other such declarations, 'there is an implicit presumption . . . that the underlying ethical claims will survive open and informed scrutiny.'[23] It follows that human rights are '*not* . . . putative legal claims'[24] although it is clear that 'the idea of moral rights can serve, and has often served in practice, as the basis of new legislation.'[25] The remit of human rights is not set in stone: 'The admissibility of a domain of continued dispute is no embarrassment to a theory of human rights.'[26] Sen continues:

> In practical applications of human rights, such debates are,
> of course, quite common and entirely customary,
> particularly among human rights activists. What is being
> argued here is that the possibility of such debates – without
> losing the basic recognition of the importance of human

---

[22] 32 *Philosophy and Public Affairs* (2004) 315.   [23] *Ibid.* p. 320
[24] *Ibid.* p. 321.   [25] *Ibid.* p. 327.   [26] *Ibid.* pp. 322–3.

rights – is not just a feature of what can be called human rights *practice*, they are actually part of the general *discipline* of human rights including the underlying theory (rather than being an embarrassment to that discipline). An acknowledgement of the necessity to pay ethical attention to human rights, far from obliterating the need for such deliberation, actually invites it. A theory of human rights can, therefore, allow considerable internal variations, without losing the commonality of the agreed principle of attaching substantial importance to human rights (and to the corresponding freedoms and obligations) and of being committed to considering seriously how that importance should be appropriately reflected.[27]

This is a truly sophisticated approach, one which seeks to turn to foundational effect the commitment to discussion that is, as we have seen, such a feature of (post-) modern philosophical thinking. But a price does have to be paid, from the objective truth point of view. Look at the last sentence here: the agreed position is not to defend, vindicate etc. but rather (merely?) to 'attach substantial importance to' human rights and 'to considering seriously how that importance should be appropriately reflected'. As Sen remarks a little later, '[t]here have to be some "threshold conditions" of (i) importance and (ii) social influenceability for a freedom to figure within the interpersonal and interactive spectrum of human rights.'[28] In practice what this means is that the duties imposed by human rights are not duties of 'absolute obligation' to act but rather require the 'giving [of] reasonable consideration to a possible action', in

[27] *Ibid.* p. 323.   [28] *Ibid.* p. 329.

other words a dialogue with the self rather than an imperative drawn from the 'true' world outside.[29] So, '[e]ven though the acknowledgement that certain freedoms qualify as human rights already reflects an assessment of their general importance and their possible influenceability . . . , a person has to go beyond these pervasive features into more specific circumstances in giving reasonable consideration to what he or she, in particular, should do in a specific case.'[30]

Now this is only partly satisfactory for a human rights activist: it is a passive foundationalism, one that is rooted in thinking not action. The power of the theory as a basis for human rights depends on a hidden assumption, namely that – having had the dialogue with the self – the individual will conclude that he or she is under a duty to act and that therefore he or she will indeed act. Consider the 'concrete example' used by Sen to illustrate 'the distinction between [these] different kinds of obligations'. It is a real-life case that occurred in Queens, New York, in 1964, 'when a woman, Kitty Genovese, was fatally assaulted in full view of many others watching the event from their apartments, who did nothing to help her':[31]

> It is plausible to argue that three terrible things happened here, which are distinct but interrelated:
> (1) the woman's freedom – and right – not to be assaulted and killed was violated (this is clearly the principle nastiness in this case);
> (2) the murderer violated the immunity that anyone should have against assault and killing (a violation of 'perfect obligation'); and

---

[29] *Ibid.* p. 339.   [30] *Ibid.*   [31] *Ibid.* p. 341.

(3) the others who *did* nothing whatever to help the victim also transgressed their general – and 'imperfect' – obligation *to seriously consider* providing the help which they could reasonably be expected to provide.[32]

I want to concentrate on the third of these positions. Note the words I have emphasised. How does Sen know that the witnesses did not 'seriously consider' whether to act, and actually decided against? He is assuming that there was no debate in their heads because he can contemplate only one outcome from such a discussion, namely action. Sen's theory is a foundationalist ethic disguised in contemporary jargon, an old-fashioned moral view of the world dressed in the new-fangled fashion that everybody is wearing these days.

Returning to basics

I have concentrated on Sen because I see him as emblematic in the drift of foundationalism from truth to discovery that has been occurring in recent years. Let me sum up what I have been saying thus far. Human rights as an idea has been exposed by the collapse in the authority first of religion and then of reason. The intellectual vacuum left open by these developments has been filled by a new kind of pseudo-foundationalism, one that seeks to turn debate, dialogue, deliberation and consequent agreement about words into a modern form of truth. But there is nothing basic here, nothing that reaches beyond words to demand that as a matter of obligation

[32] *Ibid.*

certain words must be agreed to mean a certain set of things, producing a particular set of right outcomes. There is nothing that allows us to say 'You have got to do this' in the endless deliberation that now seems the best we can hope for; to echo Ronald Dworkin's marvellous metaphor there is no 'trump' that can win the hand, ending the play in favour of something tangible called human dignity.[33] This brand of ethics delivers a certainty amenable only to those who draw their truths from the crowd. But if this is indeed not sufficiently robust for us, and surely it ought not to be, where does this leave the term 'human rights'? We cannot unlearn the scepticism about truth that has made our previous position no longer tenable. The easy answer would be to disagree with Sen and to confine human rights exclusively to the legal sphere, to say that the term can only mean the values encapsulated in documentary form in international, regional and national legal agreements, as interpreted by decision-makers and, at a later remove where there has been a dispute, the courts. But this is a very narrow approach that fails to capture what many people, perhaps most, mean today when they refer to 'human rights'. The words can be made to do more work, to reach a wider shared meaning beyond what has been reduced to legal form, but a shared meaning that has a universalist set of observations at its core, driving what that meaning should be.

It is time to return to Darwin, not for refutation this time but for a kind of secular salvation. Let us take at face value the Darwinian breakthrough that we are not in any special, immaterial way different from the other species with which we

---

[33] R. Dworkin, 'Rights as Trumps', in J. Waldron (ed.), *Theories of Rights* (Oxford University Press, Oxford, 1984). See also R. Dworkin, *Taking Rights Seriously* (Gerald Duckworth & Co, London, 1978) esp. ch. 7.

share the planet. What are the particular features that this 'clever animal' the human has, over and above the other animals also to be found here? Three in particular come to mind: first, this animal is self-conscious, capable of critical reflection of itself and where it fits in the environment in which it finds itself. Secondly, it is aware of death, both generally and specifically with regard to its own individual self. Third, this animal is capable of a set of contradictory impulses the import of which, because it is a self-conscious being, it understands: on the one hand there is the capacity for acts of compassion, hospitality and kindliness, on the other for cruelty, humiliation and callousness. Recent work on evolution has recovered this tension in Darwin, one that has for too long been obscured by the unattractive propaganda of the social Darwinists in favour of a perspective rooted entirely in the 'survival of the fittest'.[34] These days however, it is increasingly acknowledged that 'goodwill and collaboration are as much part of the human condition as ill-will and competition' and that what is really involved in evolution is 'a constant struggle, not for existence itself, but between selfishness and altruism – a struggle that neither can win.'[35]

Looked at from the victim's point of view, the consequence of cruel, humiliating and callous action is indeed shared with the animals. But it is surely revealing that the term

[34] See R.L. Cairneiro (ed.), *The Evolution of Society. Selections from Herbert Spencer's Principles of Sociology* (University of Chicago Press, Chicago, 1967).

[35] Both quotes are taken from 'The Story of Man' *The Economist* 24 December 2005–6 January 2006, p. 9. That issue of the magazine contains an excellent and highly accessible account of recent developments in the theory of evolution. See also M. Ridley, *The Origins of Virtue* (Penguin Books, London, 1996).

'inhuman' is often used to describe the results of this kind of cruelty, as are others words and phrases like 'torture' and 'degrading treatment'. These terms spring to mind when we are trying to describe how much more demeaning this pain is for us as humans than are other kinds of (non-callously inflicted) pain – where we are indeed much more on a par with the animals. Searching in an uncharacteristic way for essentials, the celebrated philosopher Richard Rorty has written that 'there is something within human beings which deserves respect and protection quite independently of the language they speak. It suggests a non-linguistic ability, the ability to feel pain, is what is important, and that differences in vocabulary are much less important'.[36] Certainly the ability to feel pain is not linguistic in a narrow sense of the term: it requires no words to make it the case. But does it follow that because pain is non-linguistic, it can have no language? Rorty certainly thinks so: 'victims of cruelty, people who are suffering, do not have much in the way of a language. There is no such thing as the "voice of the oppressed" or "the language of the victims".'[37] Here I disagree. There is such a language, the language of human rights, a language that speaks for people and that manages, by forcing people to be visible to everyone, first to make it possible for others to speak on their behalf, and then for them to speak for themselves.

Giving voice to the victims of cruelty and humiliation is a core task of these human-rights-oriented forms of communication, but – as we saw in chapter 1 – the discourse is not restricted to this, or even to human suffering in general. It is

---

[36] Rorty, *Contingency, Irony, and Solidarity* n. 12 above, p. 88.
[37] *Ibid.*, p. 94.

also a language of hospitality and of kindliness, and above all of compassion. Here is a word – compassion – that best captures the kind of active concern for others that the term 'human rights' has come to signify and which gives it more reach than an exclusive emphasis on suffering would suggest. Compassion is the term upon which our modern human rights vocabulary can be most effectively built. I owe a debt of gratitude to Professor Oliver Davies from King's College London for the work he has done in this area, in particular in his path-breaking Aquinas Lecture, delivered in 2005.[38] For Davies, compassion is neither love nor mercy; it has, quoting Martha Nussbaum, a cognitive element (understanding the other), an affective element (feeling for the other) and a voluntarist element (doing something about the other).[39] Davies observes that there 'is something subversive, indiscriminate and boundary-crossing about compassion' and he is right about this – it is through the rallying power of compassion that we can use human rights to frame and mobilize responses to suffering and to atrocities. But compassion is more than just another good thing among many. In particular it is not

> properly speaking a virtue to be practised among others.
> There is no one identifiable act that is compassionate
> (such as forgiveness, or almsgiving, or visiting the sick);
> rather all good acts towards others can be said to be
> compassionate to the extent that they embody an
> intentionality which recognises the suffering of another, is
> moved by it and seeks to relieve it, if at all possible.
> Compassion then is a virtuous disposition which

[38] 'Divine Silence, Human Rights' (copy with author).
[39] *Ibid.* ms p. 8. See M. Nussbaum, *Upheavals of Thought: The Intelligence of Emotions* (Cambridge University Press, Cambridge, 2001), esp. Part II.

underlies virtue but is not to be identified with it
tout court.[40]

On this view, compassion is a universalistic disposition from which virtue flows and the linguistic medium through which it expresses itself in the contemporary world is the language of human rights, the Esperanto of the virtuous. True, Davies and others root their ideas of compassion in religious discourses, in Davies's case that of the Catholic intellectual Thomas Aquinas and his concept of synderesis,[41] in others (for example) in the underlying basis for Buddhist ethics.[42] But the concept does not need a religious foundation in order to do good work, and it is this that makes it attractive to deploy in the human rights field.

The concentration of compassion is clearly on the particular, and this makes it especially compatible with the emphasis on the individual case that is, as we have seen, a central characteristic of human rights. However, there is a problem that now comes into view. I mentioned this in passing in chapter 1. It is undeniably an attractive feature of human rights that it is so driven by the 'human', by the specific individual case. But this narrow focus might also be thought to be a kind of weakness, denuding our subject of political power by

---

[40] Davies, 'Divine Silence, Human Rights', pp. 8–9.

[41] And cf. *Deus Caritas Est* Encyclical Letter of Pope Benedict XVI, 25 December 2005.

[42] See M. Batchelor (ed.), *The Path of Compassion. The Bodhisattva Precepts* (Altamira Press, Walnut Creek, 2004). Also of great interest is M. Vanden Eynde, 'Reflections on Martha Nussbaum's Work on Compassion from a Buddhist Perspective' 11 *Journal of Buddhist Ethics* (2004) 46.

turning it into a branch of philanthropy. There are two points in issue here: how can we build on this basic idea of compassion to get a wider set of moral engagements with the world around us than the notion of compassion would seem to entail; in other words how can we get the idea to be about more than just not being cruel to people and giving this or that hungry person you happen to bump into some food to eat – it has to be more than this because, as we have seen, international human rights law and the use of the term human rights in our political discourse aims much higher than such minimally decent acts and to leave things at this level would be unduly to inhibit the breadth of our term. Secondly, after we have constructed a wider understanding of compassion, one that is more in accord with the work in our culture that we are now saying the phrase human rights has to do, how do we get away from the specific and build a political programme without losing the particularity that we are clear is the essence of our subject?

The second of these questions is a vital one for the achievability and the subsequent sustainability of a human rights culture. It involves us in re-connecting our subject with representative democracy. This is the political theory that is built on exactly the same foundation as human rights (equality of esteem) but which has drifted away from the subject in the years that have gone by since their radical and highly effective partnership in the eighteenth century. The subject is sufficiently important to warrant separate treatment, and I will return to it in the next chapter. The first question is one that we do need to clear up before proceeding further. I have smuggled in the term compassion under cover of some observations about our basic animal capacity to cause harm and suffering and at the same time our human ability (one that we may share with some animals) to know we can do such things and to believe that it is wrong (not in our evolutionary interests?) to do them. But of course the term 'compassion' reaches rather further than this, into more human activity than mere forbearance from cruelty (hardly an activity at all). The way in which I am using the word compassion here is wider than is usual when the term is deployed today, in that (as we have seen) I am making it entail more than mere pity and am insisting on action as well as a caring state of mind. The idea is still within the range of basic human actions which are part of our evolutionary story. How do we flesh out further what we mean by compassion, so as to make it connect more with what observation tells us the term 'human rights' usually entails today? I mentioned equality of esteem in passing a moment ago: this is the bridge that leads us to a fuller set of principles. The reason we are interested in human rights to start with, and why we are looking for foundations in the first place, is because of our commitment to this kind of equality: we discussed this in chapter 1. And, as we have also seen in that earlier chapter, talk of esteem takes us inevitably to the notion of individual human dignity. These are the terms that can help us to bolster the content of our basic building block, compassion, so that it can retain its important status as a fundamental idea but can also at the same time grow a thicker human rights content than we have so far been able to give it.

The work of the distinguished philosopher James Griffin becomes very helpful at this point. Griffin sees human dignity 'as the valuable status protected by human rights.'[43] At the very core of such dignity is 'our capacity to reflect on, to choose, and to pursue what we ourselves decide is a good life'.[44] Griffin continues:

> To be an agent, in the fullest sense of which we are
> capable, one must (first) choose one's own course through
> life – that is, not be dominated or controlled by someone
> or something else (autonomy). And one's choice must also
> be real; one must (second) have at least a certain
> minimum education and information and the chance to
> learn what others think. But having chosen one's course
> one must then (third) be able to follow it; that is, one
> must have at least the minimum material . . . of resources
> and capabilities that it takes. And none of that is any good
> if someone then blocks one; so (fourth) others must also
> not stop one from pursuing what one sees as a good life
> (liberty).[45]

There is much that is valuable in Griffin's subsequent discussion of how these values of personhood manifest themselves in suitably determinate human rights. We do not need to pursue that pathway because we are not now searching for the kind of philosophical basis for human rights that Griffin seeks to supply. The same is true of the philosopher A.C. Grayling's

[43] J. Griffin, 'Discrepancies Between the Best Philosophical Account of Human Rights and the International Law of Human Rights' *Proceedings of the Aristotelian Society* (2001); J. Griffin, 'First Steps in an Account of Human Rights' 9 *European Journal of Philosophy* (2001) pp. 306–27. The quotes in the text are from John Tasioulas's excellent critique: 'Human Rights, Universality and the Values of Personhood: Retracing Griffin's Steps' 10 *European Journal of Philosophy* (2002) 79, p. 83.

[44] Griffin, 'First Steps', p. 319.   [45] *Ibid.*, p. 311.

contribution to the discussion, in a public lecture at the British Institute of Human Rights on 11 October 2005.[46] To Grayling, one can deduce from the human rights documents an assumption as to a certain way of life, one in which people 'have the opportunity to seek goods that they recognise as such, and which they choose for themselves as worthy objects of pursuit'. We all want the 'chance to make the good life for ourselves'. This sounds very much like what we mean today when we talk about human rights.

Our goal is to fill out our idea of what compassion entails so as to get from it more than individual acts of charity and the like, and thereby to get it to resemble the language of the oppressed, the down-trodden and the marginalised, in other words the discourse that I have said here is the true basis of human rights. But it is also to get it away from an exclusive concentration on the negative and towards the positive, to focus on that part of human rights that insists on making things better as well as on stopping things from getting worse. Taking our cue from Griffin and Grayling, it is not too large a leap from acting to feed a stranger to asking how his or her life can be made more successful than it is: the distinction is one first of imagination and secondly of degree, but not at all of kind. Oliver Davies was writing of the Catholic church when he asked the question, 'How can we avoid making a speech about compassion simply another particularist or exclusivist voice in the public exchange of such voices as "points of view"?', but his answer would seem to apply as directly to the

---

[46] See BIHR Brief Winter 2005, pp. 11–13 from which the quotations in the text are drawn.

human rights activist as it does to his target audience. To Davies what is important is a 'willingness to act as a medium, to undertake a voice-bearing mission, in order to make publicly present the subjectivity or perspectives of those who fall outside the domain of public debate by reason of their social marginality.'[47] Similarly those committed to human rights should acknowledge that it falls to them 'to "give voice" to the perspectives and therefore interests of the poor and disadvantaged in national society as well as those outside that society who may be negatively affected by the economic or political decisions made by powerful national governments.'[48]

We can see, therefore, that the 'unconditional hospitality' (Derrida's phrase[49]) that flows from compassion is wider, richer and more enabling than mere kindness, pity and tolerance. It is about enjoying and enabling the other to thrive rather than simply bearing with him or her. There is more here than forbearance from cruelty and humiliation, important though such conscious restraint is. There is also more than the occasional act of pity or kindness. Rooted in an imaginative understanding of what compassion can be made to entail, this human rights language asserts that we are all equal in view of our humanity and that our dignity, rooted in wonder at the brute fact of our achievement, demands that we each of us be given the chance to do the best we can, to thrive, to flourish, to do something with ourselves. Remembering Darwin we must note not only that this is increasingly seen as part of what successful evolution is all

[47] Davies, 'Divine Silence, Human Rights', p. 15.   [48] *Ibid.*
[49] Derrida in Borradori, *Philosophy in a Time of Terror* n. 1 above, p. 129.

about, but also that a commitment to dignity and compassion does not necessarily involve a religious insight of any sort: 'the emergence of the human being even as a matter of chance in a blind cosmos is a genuine cause for wonder; and the product of the human species in the course of evolution is something to be wondered at with something approaching awe, or natural reverence.'[50]

With this work done we are in a position to take on the key challenge of building a political programme. The translation of our personal commitment to this robust version of compassion into a political ideology is, as I shall argue in chapter 3, only achievable through democracy. Democracy is part of human rights because it is the best way we have yet found of reflecting our inherent equality in the political arena. Moral progress is measured by how seriously we work through the insight that we are all equal, how much of a chance we give to each of us to grow as we choose, even where the growing is not of the sort we would choose to do. Freedom and respect for human rights involve at bottom a recognition of the contingency that is inherent in all our efforts to tie down words and ways of living, a rejection of right answers in search of the chance to develop as best we can. Schumpeter was right when he said that 'to realise the relative validity of one's convictions and yet stand for them unflinchingly' was what 'distinguishes a civilised man from a barbarian.'[51] (There are limits of course, but these are for chapter 4, on the crisis of national security.) But once all this is realised pluralism's shelter is much less leaky that we first imagined.

---

[50] Mahoney, *Challenge of Human Rights* n. 4 above, p. 163.
[51] Quoted by Rorty, *Contingency, Irony, and Solidarity* n. 12 above, p. 46.

Rights and utility

Do we need the language of human rights for all this? Some would argue that an approach to society rooted in utilitarianism, in a commitment to happiness, does all the work that is required in this area, and that there is no need to fall back on contrived moral obligations like human rights. This was of course Jeremy Bentham's position when he launched the famous broadside against the French Declaration of the Rights of Man which I have discussed earlier in this chapter. Happiness has enjoyed something of a renaissance recently, with a powerful new protagonist having emerged from the ranks of academe to put its case with energy and enthusiasm. This is my colleague at LSE, the distinguished economist Professor Lord Richard Layard.[52] Layard's brand of utility is committed to 'a society in which people are as happy as possible and in which each person's happiness counts equally'. He wants to replace the 'intense individualism' which is such a feature of society today but which has, he says, manifestly 'failed to make us happier'. But to what extent does his focus on (personal) happiness escape this individualistic trap? Here are Layard's 'key factors affecting a person's happiness':

> Family and personal life come top in every study, and work and community life rank high. Health and freedom are also crucial, and money counts too, but in a very specific way.

[52] R. Layard, *Happiness: Lessons from a New Science* (Allen Lane, London, 2005). See also his concise summary of his thesis, 'Happiness is Back', in *Prospect* March 2005, pp. 22–26. The quotes from Layard's work that follow are drawn from the *Prospect* essay.

True, there is a reference to family here but not much else separate from the self, and certainly nothing about the outsider, the neighbour even. Layard sets his utilitarianism up in opposition to contemporary culture, but it is surely closer to what he attacks than he allows:

> We live in an age of unprecedented individualism. The highest obligation many people feel is to make the most of themselves, to realise their potential. This is a terrifying and lonely objective. Of course they feel obligations to other people too, but these are not based on any clear set of ideas. The old religious worldview is gone; so too is the postwar religion of social and national solidarity. We are left with no concept of the common good or collective meaning.

I agree with all this but am not at all clear how utility, with its emphasis on personal (and – at a stretch – family) happiness can possibly be the answer. Where is its 'common good' or social bond with which to re-achieve 'social and national solidarity'? The respect to which utility is committed is self-respect, not respect of others. As Layard says, 'what people most want is respect. They seek economic status because it brings respect.'

Now of course Layard is too humane a scholar to think that this is enough to meet the problems of individualism that he has identified. Mindful of this, he has a whole menu of things that we *ought* to favour because they will make us happier:

> We should respect people who co-operate with others at no gain to themselves . . .

> We should be sceptical of institutions which give greater
> weight to rank, such as performance-related pay . . .
>
> If we want a happier society, we should focus most on
> the experiences which people value for their intrinsic
> worth and not because other people have them – above
> all, on relationships in the family, at work and in the
> community.

Most importantly, there is the risk that we might not only be
happy by focusing on ourselves but might make ourselves even
happier by handing out some tough treatment to others to
whom we are indifferent. Layard's solution to this problem is
curiously at odds with his starting point:

> I would . . . give extra weight to improving the happiness
> of those who are least happy, thus ruling out the
> oppression of minorities. (This also deals with the
> superficial objection to utilitarianism that it would
> vindicate the brutal abuse of a small minority if such
> abuse made the majority happier.)

But how superficial is this objection? It must look pretty fundamental to those whose lives are sacrificed pursuant to some
communally agreed goal (ethnic purity; national solidarity)
that makes most people happier most of the time. But at this
stage in his argument, Layard's approach to happiness seems to
have become so prescriptive, so determined to explain to
people how best they can be happy, and to insist that he knows
the route to happiness that they ought to be obliged to take,
that it has moved well beyond his starting point of personal
happiness, so much so that it has become in fact – if not in
words – a theory of human rights. It is human rights not

happiness that explains why we ought to strive for the various outcomes of which Layard approves: respect for others, concern for minorities, empathy with the stranger, concern for the community and so on. He is a moral philosopher pretending to be merely scientific and descriptive:

> To become happier, we have to change our inner attitudes as much as our outward circumstances. I am talking of the perennial philosophy which enables us to find the positive side in others. Such compassion to ourselves and others, can be learned.

Indeed it can. It is called a human rights education.

Rights and liberal irony

There is another response to Layard's last remark which says it is not a human rights but rather a 'sentimental' education that we need. With these liberal ironists we might say that 'recognition of a common susceptibility to humiliation is the *only* social bond that is needed'[53] and that our 'sense of human solidarity is based on a sense of a common danger, not a common possession or a shared power'.[54] On this view the individual 'thinks that what unites [him or] her with the rest of the species is not a common language but *just* susceptibility to pain and in particular to that special sort of pain which the brutes do not share with the humans – humiliation.'[55] The 'notion of "inalienable human rights" is no better and no worse a slogan than that of "obedience to the will of God." '[56]

---

[53] Rorty, *Contingency, Irony, and Solidarity* n. 12 above, p. 91.   [54] *Ibid.*
[55] *Ibid.* p. 92.   [56] Rorty, *Philosophy and Social Hope* n. 11 above, p. 83.

To the doyen of the liberal ironists Richard Rorty, 'human rights are superstitions – contrivances put forward by the weak to protect themselves against the strong.'[57]

Let us pause to reflect on this idea of human rights as 'a superstition'. As I have now said, perhaps too many times, the phrase 'human rights' hinges on equality of respect and this is the idea which is in turn the lynchpin of democracy, making sense of the otherwise bizarre notion that everybody should have an equal say in the running of their community, regardless of their family connections, wealth, intelligence and so on. To Rorty, a 'liberal society is one whose ideals can be fulfilled by persuasion rather than force, by reform rather than revolution, by the free and open encounters of present linguistic and other practices with suggestions for new practices.'[58] But it is clear that this kind of liberal society cannot be taken for granted in the present age: it is under attack from various enemies, economic power, fundamentalist religion, national exclusivity among them. Rorty has himself written an almost alarmist essay to this effect.[59] The flip-side of liberalism, the commitment to compassion over cruelty and to personal flourishing over public prejudice, is also more exposed than it has been since the pluralist view of the world first grabbed our imagination and persuaded us of its truth. Our democratic and legal processes are already in severe danger of being captured by the rich, while our public culture is increasingly filled with the noise of demonising rabble-rousers. With what can liberal society fight back? Religious words don't work anymore, and

---

[57] *Ibid.* p. 84.
[58] Rorty, *Contingency, Irony, and Solidarity* n. 12 above, p. 60.
[59] 'Post Democracy' 26 *London Review of Books* (2004) no. 7 (1 April).

talk of rationally based moral obligation is also beside the point. Socialism is in a quiescent phase. Even social democrats are losing confidence. And the liberal ironist wants us also to change the subject when 'human rights' come up? I think this is going too far: post-modern decency needs to grab help where it can find it, without being too picky about origins.

In this current age of doubt, with cruelty abundant in the gaps left in our culture by the abandonment of all our truths, and with the retreat of our soldiers of certainty swelling into a panicked stampede, we have reached the point where we should now admit that human kind simply cannot cope with too much unreality. We need truths – especially if they are true but also even if we have to make them up. It is not enough to leave everything to sentiment – our better selves need more help than a few recommended readings, a movie or two and a deft capacity to dodge unpleasant conversations. Our culture is simply not up to jettisoning so much of the past while holding out such intangible and unsupported hope for the future. And if the good guys give up on the language of human rights, then others – less principled, differently motivated – will fill the words with a bleaker kind of meaning, ridiculing their preposterous breadth perhaps, or using the term to justify killing foreigners with differently coloured skins (in the name of securing their human rights, no doubt). The phrase 'human rights' will not disappear if over-scrupulous liberals refuse to have anything to do with it: the words exist, they can be made to do good work: the pragmatist should embrace the phrase and make it work, not wander from the battlefield of meaning with intellectual purity intact but honour in shreds.

The term 'human rights' is the phrase we use when we

56

are trying to describe decency in our post-philosophical world. It provides a link with the better parts of our past while guiding us towards the finer features of our future. To paraphrase Oliver Wendall Holmes, this is a kind of thinking that works – it gives pithy expression to our feeling that there should be less cruelty and is a handy way of saying what many of us feel, that everybody should be given a chance to do the best they can in life. It is the term that at the present time best fits the evolutionary insight that to progress the human species needs kindliness, compassion and hospitality as well as the baser survival instincts of the (only ostensibly) fittest. And if we can agree on this meaning for human rights, then we can spot bad-faith, the guy who wants to kill a community so as to secure its freedom; the political leaders who think they can create a human rights culture in a community where half the people are impoverished; the professor who feels a little bit of roughing up is necessary to protect human rights.

Alastair MacIntyre may well have been right when he said that '[n]atural or human rights ... are fictions'.[60] Certainly he was if we think back to the way in which the term 'human rights' has historically been used, as a way of articulating religious or rationally deduced moral obligations. Much of the power of modern philosophical work has lain in the exposure of fictions such as these. As MacIntyre put it 'Unmasking the unacknowledged motives of arbitrary will and desire which sustain the moral masks of modernity is itself one of the most characteristically modern of activities.'[61] I have tried to locate the essence of these insights in

---

[60] MacIntyre, *After Virtue* n. 18 above, p. 70.
[61] *Ibid.* p. 72. Emphasis in the original.

some fundamentals about the species, using Darwin as my unlikely, universalist saviour. But even if this does not persuade you, it does not necessarily follow that for this reason alone you should reject my narrative – to believers I say, 'I am glad that together we have found some universal truths, rooted in a particular reading of Darwin, which we can now call by the name of "human rights"'; to the sceptics I say, 'forget the weaknesses in the argument and look at the attractive ethical and political programmes that result'. It follows that for the sceptics I say that I think the time has come for some strategic remasking. I think MacIntyre was wrong to hanker after a now impossible Aristotelian virtue but he was right that something needs to be done. That something is the construction of a remasked self, someone who might not be persuaded by my Darwinian universalism, who knows the contingency of language and the limitations it imposes on the search for truth, knows the uncertainty of all claims to knowledge, believes that there is no core self but rather layers of accidentally accrued identity, but who nevertheless embraces goodness and dignity and right and wrong as words that – despite everything – work to make the world a better place.

I end by returning to Richard Rorty's word 'superstition'. Of course the term 'human rights' is a superstition; it can be nothing else in the world of language that the term is forced to inhabit. But a superstition is not necessarily a myth and it is certainly not bound to be a lie. A mask can hide a face but it may be an exact resemblance to what is underneath. Maybe I am right about my Darwinian universals, maybe I am not. We just don't know – all we can be sure of is that just because we have made something up it does not necessarily follow that –

out there beyond words – it is not true. I end this chapter with what I think of as a great human rights poem, by Les Murray the Australian poet:

THE MEANING OF EXISTENCE

Everything except language
knows the meaning of existence.
Trees, planets, rivers, time
know nothing else. They express it
moment by moment as the universe.

Even this fool of a body
lives it in part, and would
have full dignity within it
but for the ignorant freedom
of my talking mind.

3

The crisis of legalism

A reason why I was keen in chapter 2 to get under the skin of human rights and to develop an ethical base for the subject that could survive scrutiny was that I feared that without such a foundation the subject would be all the more vulnerable to other challenges, other threats to its survival. In this and the next chapter I look at two such hazards, each in its own way a consequence of the success that, as I have already recognised, the subject undoubtedly enjoys today. In chapter 4, I will look at how the term 'human rights' has come to be abused by the powerful, as a means of legitimising the exploitation both of peoples and of the world's natural resources. In that chapter, I will ask what can we do to protect 'human rights' from being captured by those who would use it in this way to mask other, more brutal projects, such as colonial-style militarism or the abuse of persons within their power. This chapter takes a different tack. When I was talking in the last chapter about rooting the human rights idea in an active sense of compassion, I raised then the danger that this approach, laudatory though it is, would not translate well into the political sphere, and that as a result human rights as a subject would never outgrow its individual-oriented, person-focused origins. My worry was that our subject would remain stuck in philanthropy and altruism, forever dealing with a succession of single cases, and would never be able to broaden and deepen sufficiently to reach the whole

community, thereby achieving effective change via a programme of political action.

This chapter is concerned with the key question of how
human rights can be embedded in society as a set of realistic
and achievable political goals and not just as a guide to good
behaviour in individual cases. A curious feature of the human
rights movement has been that the answer to this question has
largely been seen to lie with legal codification rather than with
direct and sustained political action. My main focus, therefore,
flowing from the way that I deal with this first issue, will be with
the opportunities this legal pathway offers us. But it will also be
with the dangers inherent in the successful entrenching of the
term 'human rights' in law and legal discourse, and how to
counter or reduce these hazards. Because the points I will be
making about human rights as a legal programme fit particularly well with democratic countries, I will be concerned chiefly
with the way in which the idea of human rights is treated in the
domestic legal systems of such countries rather than with the
world as a whole. And because the nation state is still firmly our
first port of call for legal and indeed political matters, with
proper legal implementation still being largely the preserve of
national rather than international law, I will be mainly interested in analysing the effect of domestic (rather than international) human rights law on these democratic polities. So my
reflections in this chapter on the democratic and legal sides to
human rights may strike some of you as unambitious, provincial even. To such potentially disappointed readers, I can only
plead that you bear with me: many of the points I raise
here would apply equally to international law and to international governance, if either were as sophisticated as national

61

systems – with some 400 years of experience behind them – now are.[1] So while I agree that this chapter tackles the local problems of today, they are issues that have the potential to become – if democratic cosmopolitanism really takes hold – the challenges of tomorrow as well.[2]

The dangerous triumph of legal enforceability

Every idea jostling in the political firmament seeks the campaigning jackpot of legal implementation. A point of view has really triumphed when it has shed its activist personality and turned the state – with its executive, its judges, its lawyers, its police force – from adversaries into allies, powerful enforcers of what not so long ago had been way beyond their field of vision, a speck on the periphery of political discussion. Thus it is with human rights. Ideas about compassion and the avoidance of cruelty have an individual focus, but they have also been able to muster an impressive head-of-steam behind them. What has been especially remarkable has been the way in which these basic ideas have been so speedily translated into a set of practical entitlements which have then been described as applicable to all and which are furthermore said to be untrammelled by any jurisdictional or utilitarian calculus. The first shape that these ethical commitments have so successfully assumed has been in a field that as I have already said will not

[1] See A.J. Langlois, 'Human Rights without Democracy? A Critique of the Separationist Thesis' 25 *Human Rights Quarterly* (2003) 990.

[2] See *A More Secure World: Our Shared Responsibility. Report of the High Level Panel on Threats, Challenges and Change* (UN, A/59/565, December 2004), esp. ch. 18.

detain us long here, that of international human rights law. We looked briefly at the rise of this subject in chapter 2.[3] We saw there that the momentum driving forward these human rights ideas has been such that they have not lingered long in the sphere of mere ideas before being repackaged as international law entitlements. There was the Universal Declaration on Human Rights in 1948 and then the two Covenants in 1966 and much else of a legal or quasi-legal nature ever since. The simple but important point about all this for present purposes is that right from the start of its post-World War II renaissance, the success of the human rights project has been measured in terms of its reach into codes of (international) law.

It is not surprising that human rights should seek to identify itself in the international arena in terms of law and legal enforceability: as I noted a moment ago there is no universal democratic culture, rooted in the United Nations or elsewhere, into which the energies of our subject could be successfully directed. This is not the case with democratic states. These have by definition a lively civic space in which discussion, dialogue and debate take priority over the legal. Despite this, and mimicking the international codes that have been developed since 1948, the human rights idea in these more local contexts has also invariably found its ambitions and its political programmes being defined in highly generalised legal forms, more concrete than simple statements about compassion and cruelty to be sure but pretty vague nevertheless. Over the past twenty-five years, and particularly since the end of the Cold War, a commitment to judicially

---

[3] See pp. 25–28 above.

enforceable bills of rights has quite quickly become part of
the legal mainstream in all democracies, even in those places
whose deep democratic pedigrees might have been expected
to have insulated them from this new human rights wave.[4]
The United States has long had its own indigenous code of
human rights, of course, in the form of the Bill of Rights
promulgated as a set of amendments to its constitution. But
now Canada,[5] New Zealand,[6] and many of the European
countries such as Sweden[7] and Ireland[8] have embraced bills
of rights. Post-colonial states have invariably taken the same
road, with the most dramatic example being found in South
Africa's post-apartheid constitution.[9] The European Convention on Human Rights – replete with very general rights
claims of various shapes and sizes – has been the driving
force in wedding newly emerging post-Soviet Bloc states to
the legal form of a general set of human rights guarantees.
Not even that most established of elective democracies, the
United Kingdom, has been immune to the Convention tide,
with each of its constituent parts being required to abide

---

[4] M.R. Ishay, *The History of Human Rights. From Ancient Times to the
Globalization Era* (University of California Press, Berkeley, 2004),
esp. chs. 4 and 6.

[5] Canadian Charter of Rights and Freedoms (Part I Constitution Act
1982). [6] New Zealand Bill of Rights Act 1990.

[7] On which see generally I. Cameron, 'Sweden' in C.A. Gearty (ed.),
European Civil Liberties and the European Convention on Human Rights
(Martinus Nijhoff, The Hague, 1997), ch. 6.

[8] European Convention on Human Rights Act 2003.

[9] Constitution of the Republic of South Africa 1996. See also the
earlier Constitution of India (Part III, 'Fundamental Rights', Arts.
12–35).

by human rights law and with the Kingdom as a whole being also bound, since 2 October 2000, by the terms of the Human Rights Act 1998. Australia is now one of the last remaining democracies where rights are not to be found and even here resistance is crumbling fast.[10]

It is clear, therefore, that whatever one says about its ethical origins, we can now be confident that the idea of human rights involves rather more than sporadic acts of charity, pity or hospitality. Its basic commitment to human dignity and to equality of esteem, grounded (as I have argued in chapter 2) in an active sense of compassion, has been unfolded quite quickly into a political programme which has in turn equally speedily swooped upon the translation into law of certain 'fundamental' and 'inalienable' human rights as its primary political goal. This rapid prioritisation of the legal over the political – fuelled by observing the emphasis (already noted here) of the international on general codes of legal and quasi-legal rights – has been central to the way in which we have sought to develop a sustainable set of general goals for human rights, targets that lift the subject out of individual philanthropy and give it a generalised appeal. I will come back later to the different ways human rights has been introduced into domestic law: it will be a key part of my argument both that there are right and wrong ways of doing this and – to give you a sneak preview of what follows – that the UK approach

---

[10] See L. McDonald, 'New Directions in the Australian Bill of Rights Debate' [2004] *Public Law* 22; G. Williams, *Human Rights under the Australian Constitution* (Oxford University Press, Melbourne, 2002); G. Williams, *A Bill of Rights for Australia* (University of New South Wales Press, Sydney, 2000).

represents a solution whereas many of the others offer only problems – problems that are sufficiently grave to justify the claim in the title to this chapter, that human rights now faces a 'crisis of legalism'.

Before turning my attention to these negative points, however, I should take a moment to make clear that the speedy transformation of human rights into generalised human rights law can have beneficial effects. As I said at the start of this section, getting law on your side is what all activists for a particular point of view pine for, and with no little justification. The benefits are clearest of all where the previous regime in some place or other had been wholly lacking in respect for individual dignity and the rule of law. But such laws also undoubtedly help even in established democratic countries which, broadly speaking, already take a human rights approach to the government of their peoples, supplying more explicit principles than might hitherto have been found, filling gaps in the law where human rights support for the weak might otherwise have gone unnoticed, and generally helping to guide such cultures further along the paths of civility and humanity than they might otherwise have gone.[11] If we were looking for evidence of this we could point to such path-breaking decisions as the school desegregation and civil rights decisions of the US Supreme Court under Chief Justice Warren[12] and, more

---

[11] See generally as far as the United Kingdom is concerned, C.A. Gearty, *Principles of Human Rights Adjudication* (Oxford University Press, Oxford, 2004).

[12] Principally *Brown v Board of Education* 347 US 483 (1954). For the Warren Court, see B. Schwartz, *A History of the Supreme Court* (Oxford University Press, New York and Oxford, 1993), ch. 12.

recently, the case law in the UK on the human rights obligation to prevent asylum seekers from falling into destitution.[13] In chapter 2, I identified the essential utility of human rights as being its capacity to provide a language for the voiceless, the vulnerable and the marginalised in our society, those who have no other means of getting the public's attention in our post-religious, post-socialist culture. To have this voice inserted into a discourse as powerful as that of law is undoubtedly to give it fresh authority, more power, more reach, and this is the case even in reasonably functioning democracies.

But as I have already suggested the human rights story in law is not unequivocal good news. There is a Faustian bargain being struck here, a price that is being paid for so speedy a movement from the radical fringes to the established (legal) mainstream. In the political world, backed-up now I hope by the kind of philosophical work we have been doing in chapter 2, the term 'human rights' stands for progressive ideas like equality of esteem, respect for individual dignity, a commitment to human flourishing and a reduction in cruelty. It is a dynamic player in the political fray, arguing for a certain view of mankind, not afraid to take on and seek to defeat other, harsher versions of right and wrong. This is done without rancour, without the feeling that the human rights point-of-view ought not to have to compete in the political market-place. In this discourse, the claim to definitive authority implicit in the term 'human rights' is left to one side, the statement 'these are our human rights' being best understood to be

---

[13] R (Limbuela) v Secretary of State for the Home Department [2005] UKHL 66.

part of an argument rather than a revelation about our moral obligations that should – through force of its Truth – bring all discussion to an end.[14] This approach fits well with the anti-foundational mood of the times, a point upon which I elaborated at length in the last chapter.[15] It sees human rights as a lively and progressive feature of our democratic polity rather than as something outside it, bringing in non-negotiable versions of right and wrong to close the discussion down.

Where the human rights energy generated by this reform-minded politics produces particular laws focused on certain problems, its emancipatory power can be maintained through law. Legislation on the homeless,[16] for example, or on health[17] or education[18] can be clear, specific as to the duties that are required and therefore readily enforceable. In this way the rhetoric of human rights is translated into precise and carefully constructed positive rights. The law is the means through which practical applications of the human rights aspiration are made real. On this account, legal rights are the servant of the political, changing with the ebb and flow of democratic debate. These legal rights can come onto and go from the statute books without embarrassment because, whatever about the early human rights claims that got them enacted, there is no question now but that they are offshoots of the political, expressions of the passing wishes of the

---

[14] J. Feinberg, *Rights, Justice and the Bounds of Liberty. Essays in Social Philosophy* (Princeton University Press, New Jersey, 1980).

[15] See esp. the discussion of Amartya Sen, pp. 36–39.

[16] Housing (Homeless Persons) Act 1977 (UK).

[17] National Health Service Act 1946 (UK).

[18] Education Act 1944 (UK).

community. They might not even call themselves human rights. Indeed in such a political system, whether or not they are human rights to start with, they become (mere) legal rights the moment they are turned into legislation, their moral ambitions trimmed in the name of successful and practical enforceability.

General human rights laws are different. Taking their cue from the international, these measures seek to capture the power of the human rights ideal in legislation but in an abstract way. They speak in wide terms about rights to life, liberty, speech, non-discrimination, or even more ambitiously of rights to broadly defined social and economic goods (a job; social security; shelter). There is no subject-specific context: the rights are said to apply across the public service board (and perhaps also into the private sphere as well). This is the entanglement of human rights within the law that I am mainly concerned about in this chapter, the bills of rights and constitutional instruments and so on that seek to translate the abstract power of human rights straight onto legal terrain. It is these efforts that give rise to 'the crisis of legalism' to which I have referred earlier. Large-scale human rights instruments like these, particularly those planted on the summit of the law at its highest constitutional peak, may look like tremendous successes from the slopes below, especially from the base camp of politics from which the ascent necessarily commences. But my argument here is that it is a dangerous climb, one whose success can do harm to the very fabric of human rights, demoralising many of those left at base and rendering more adventurous climbs impossible in the future. For treating human rights law as sovereign in this way narrows the radical power of human rights, and reduces the emancipatory power of our subject by setting up the law in false opposition to the political. Let me be clear that I am not talking now about how this or that bill of rights is drafted or what the judges say about how it is to be enforced. In particular I am not building an argument about the dangers of the legalisation of human rights that is dependant on a succession of cases from around the world of which I disapprove and on which I hope to persuade you to share my view. The crisis of legalism is more serious than that, emerging out of the deep structure of our subject when it takes legal shape, and caused by the resulting imposition of a false division between human rights in its legal form on the one hand and, on the other, the political community from which these rights have come, and in which they must operate.

The taming of human rights

Let me explain this last point a bit further by tracing what usually happens when the politically energetic concept of 'human rights' is reduced to legal form. There are four stages in this process of legalisation. First, the generality of the term and its moral cachet in civil society invariably gives the 'protection of human rights' a very much wider reach than is the case with ordinary law: more areas of conduct are affected across a wider range of activity and a great variety of laws are required to be read subject to the dictates of human rights. This happens whenever the precision of positive rights is forsaken in favour of the grander but vaguer claims of more generally phrased 'human rights', as though the law has to make up in decibels for what it has lost in accuracy. But secondly, with the legalisation of human rights, the custodianship of the idea moves from the political to the legal sphere, from the NGOs, the MPs and so on to the judges and the lawyers. And it is their version of human rights that now matters, not that of the political activists who first promoted the idea. Nor is their legal rendering of human rights just one perspective among many. For thirdly, we must note that with its translation into the legal sphere comes a renewal in the authority of human rights.

This is a key point for the purposes of this chapter. All laws are of course designed to some degree to supplant political dispute with certainty, but the level of authority achieved by human rights law is frequently of a higher order altogether. As my first proposition made clear, in many (but not all[19]) systems it stands above other laws, dominating the whole legal framework with its clear view as to right and wrong. To return to my mountaineering metaphor, it is on the summit looking down, not just on other laws but also at the political hubbub from which the idea has so recently emerged. The superior moral status of the human rights claim, much reduced by its fight for attention among many other interests in the political marketplace, seeming then to be a mere piece of political rhetoric or a term used only in a manifesto sense,[20] is restored to preeminence by its scaling of law's tallest peak. The victory is confirmed by its re-emergence in the form of a set of constitutional or basic rights to which all laws and political activity must defer.

[19] A point to which I will return: see pp. 93–98 below.
[20] Feinberg, *Rights, Justice and the Bounds of Liberty* n. 14 above.

Embedded in the law in this powerful way, and under the command of lawyers rather than politicians, the concept of human rights recovers its moral authority, its confidence in its ability to distinguish right from wrong, to order what ought to be done 'in the name of human rights'. So far so good. But what is the nature of this new-found authority? What are the underlying truths about human rights that have been dormant within the political process, but which are now liberated by this transfer of the trusteeship of the idea from the legislative to the judicial sphere? The problem is that, fourthly, in recovering its certainty in what is right and what is wrong, and in overseeing other laws for compatibility with this brand of truth, human rights law seems invariably to find itself reverting to a particular philosophical tradition that has certainly had its uses in past generations but which is not particularly helpful or persuasive today. This is the line of thinking that essentially sees the idea of human rights not as an emancipatory political concept at all but rather as a pre- or a supra-political ideal, as reflective of a truth beyond politics to which politics ought to be subject. On this view, our core or essential human rights are made up of a number of rights that people have which *precede* politics or which are *above* politics. They are not rights which are achieved (and sustained) *through* politics.

Attractive though it is to the vanity of lawyers, appealing to their self-importance and downgrading the value of a political culture in which they play little or no part, this version of human rights is faulty, rooted in old ideas about human nature that no longer reflect what human rights is all about. It also ignores the fact that such instruments flow out of politics in the first place. There are no places out there where we can find pre-political or supra-political human rights capable of being credibly described in isolation from the community to which they belong. The assumption is bogus, part of an old foundationalist approach to human rights that has long been (or should have been) discarded in political and philosophical circles. We did some of this discarding ourselves in chapter 2. Unfortunately this perspective lives on in the legal world, where the need for authority has made the lurch to supra-political truth seem unavoidable. But it *is* an avoidable mistake and for the future health of our subject we must work hard to ensure that it is avoided. Fortunately (as I have already hinted a few pages ago) we have a precedent to hand, postulating a different kind of authority; it is one that retains the potency of the human rights label while not cutting itself adrift from the political. I will come to this solution to the crisis later in this chapter: first I must say a little more about the mistake, how it came about, and the kind of damage that it is doing.

The false dichotomy between human rights and politics

Three key figures in the development of human rights have been responsible above all others for getting us to think of human rights as somehow detached from politics. Living during the unsettled seventeenth century, Thomas Hobbes (1588–1679) was one of the first writers to think seriously about the fundamental rights of individuals. His trick was to speculate about the kinds of rights we might all have in the wholly hypothetical state of nature that he imagined preceded political society. On Hobbes's gloomy analysis, such a place would be an entirely nasty one, with each of us enjoying the right to everything and with mayhem and disorder the inevitable result. The upshot of this horrific state of nature was the emergence of a strong state, a Leviathan, to which we all agreed we needed to transfer our rights. A generation later, John Locke took Hobbes's idea of the state of nature but saw the consequent establishment of a governing authority as a safeguard for certain basic rights rather than as an obliteration of them.[21] On Locke's view, there was a need for government in order to protect the fundamental rights of man to 'life, liberty and estate': if government failed at this task of the protection of rights then its authority could perfectly legitimately be rejected by those for whom acceptance of it had always been conditional on its doing this job (of protecting human rights) properly.

The details of neither of these political philosophies need concern us here. What does matter is that each saw the idea of 'human rights' as antecedent to politics, as something that people had before their engagement with those around them led them to some kind of political settlement. On both these accounts, therefore, human rights represented a basic truth outside of politics. Hobbes saw this basic truth as requiring subjugation to state power. Locke in contrast saw our innate freedom as something which politics was designed to protect. Neither thought that human rights or freedom could come out of politics; both thought that it belonged at a deeper, truer level. This perspective on human rights was amplified by

---

[21] C.B. Macpherson, *The Political Theory of Possessive Individualism* (Oxford University Press, Oxford, 1962); J. Dunn, *Locke: A Very Short Introduction* (Oxford University Press, Oxford, 2003).

our third influential thinker, Immanuel Kant, writing a generation later. As Kant put it,

> There is nothing more sacred in the wide world than the rights of others. They are inviolable. Woe unto him who trespasses upon the right of another and tramples it underfoot! His right should be his security; it should be stronger than any shield or fortress. We have a holy ruler and the most sacred of his gifts to us is the rights of man.[22]

Together Locke and Kant give rise to a strong liberal perspective on rights. In its day this point of view did excellent emancipatory work, underpinning a move away from kingly and religious power in the direction of personal autonomy and community self-determination. The eventual success of the English revolution of the seventeenth century served further to entrench Locke's version of human rights as the common sense of successive generations of British writers, parliamentarians and thinkers. It still dominates in legal circles but I think that its benefits are now greatly exceeded by the harm that it does.

If its main problem is its location of human rights outside politics, its central weakness is its failure to think through what exactly it means to say that individuals enjoy rights in opposition to the political community. This shortcoming did not matter so much when those with such rights were the only people who made up the legislature: in such situations there was next to no tension between the two, with the decisions of the political community being bound to respect the rights of all those who made it up. But it began to matter

---

[22] Cited in R. Norman, *The Moral Philosophers: An Introduction to Ethics* (Clarendon Press, Oxford, 1983), p. 122.

a great deal when the drive towards democratic government got truly underway and it became normal to expect government to be representative of the community as a whole and not just those with property or other kinds of economic advantage. This democratic movement grew out of two sources, and neither had any time for the liberal version of rights popularised by Locke. The first was the rights-based theorising of Jean Jacques Rousseau, who saw man as an essentially free being but one that had been dragged down and crushed by the unfairness and inequality of society which had 'for the benefit of a few ambitious men subjected the human race . . . to labour, servitude and misery.'[23] According to Rousseau what was needed was a new social contract through which the general will of the whole community could be realised, thereby achieving freedom for all. The people acting together did not bring their separate human rights to their deliberations; rather it was through the process of formulating their general will that they produced freedom. Our second proto-democrat Jeremy Bentham, was less grandiloquent than Rousseau but equally certain that it was for the community as a whole to decide upon what was best, i.e. what was most likely to be conducive to the general good, to make most of them happy most of the time. To Bentham rights flowed out of the legislative process, as a result of decisions made by such a body: they did not exist in advance of their enactment.[24]

---

[23] See M. Cranston (ed.), *Jean-Jacques Rousseau, A Discourse on Inequality* (Penguin, Harmondsworth, 1984), p. 122. Apologies for the gender-specific language.

[24] J. Waldron (ed.), *'Nonsense upon Stilts': Bentham, Burke and Marx on the Rights of Man* (Methuen Press, London, 1987).

It is hard for us to recall quite how terrifying the idea of democracy was to the propertied and otherwise economically advantaged of the nineteenth-and early twentieth-century industrialised world. It was genuinely believed that the mob was about to destroy privilege in the name of equality. The idea of a political system whose laws could not infringe basic freedoms became enormously attractive to those who had these basic freedoms to lose, the 'few ambitious men' of whom Rousseau had written with such anger. Thus did the language of human rights mutate from a radical voice into an intensely reactionary one in the space of just a couple of generations. Without legalised rights, all the British judges of the time could do was snarl and cite Locke while their efforts to scupper legislative initiatives in the name of freedom fell foul of Parliament's repeated assertions of its sovereign power and its straight denial that there were any so-called rights anywhere that it could not touch.[25] In the United States, however, armed with a bill of rights incorporated into the Constitution as a basic law, the judges were able, under the disguise of a commitment to basic freedom, to debilitate progressive legislation for two generations.[26] It was not until the mid-1930s that the American federal government was sufficiently strong to act seriously for the benefit of all its people without worrying about the judges scuppering everything to protect the human or civil rights of Rousseau's 'few ambitious men'.

[25] *Amalgamated Society of Railway Servants v Osborne* [1910] AC 87, esp. the speech of Lord Shaw of Dunfermline.

[26] See M. Tushnet, *Taking the Constitution Away from the Courts* (Princeton University Press, Princeton New Jersey, 1999).

The reactionary force of human rights law was a commonplace of left-wing thinking until very recently. The perception flowed out of the way in which such law set up human rights guarantees in opposition to the democratic polity and then empowered judges (un-elected, unaccountable, unrepresentative and so on) to police the elected representatives of a people, ensuring that they behaved in a proper, human rights way, i.e. from a revolutionary or radical perspective entirely quiescently. Thus the insertion of rights guarantees in the remodelled German and Italian constitutions at the end of the Second World War was widely seen as a more or less transparent attempt to prevent the emergence of a democratically based, socialist alternative to liberal and social democracy in the defeated axis powers.[27] During the 1950s and 1960s, the decolonisation process was often accompanied by new charters of rights as the departing imperial powers sought to guarantee the position of the affluent settlers they were leaving behind. The same dynamic explained the enthusiasm for human rights displayed by the dying apartheid regime in South Africa in the late 1980s, and by the disappearing colonial regime in Hong Kong a few years later.[28] All of this was taken more or less for granted on the Left though pointing it out to legal audiences was usually guaranteed to provoke apoplexy, even at LSE.[29]

---

[27] M. Mandel, 'A Brief History of the New Constitutionalism, or "How We Changed Everything so that Everything Would Remain the Same"' 32 *Israel Law Review* (1998) 250.

[28] Hong Kong Bill of Rights Ordinance 1991.

[29] J.A.G. Griffith, 'The Political Constitution' 42 *Modern Law Review* (1979) 1; see C. Harlow, 'The Political Constitution Reworked' [2006] *New Zealand Law Review* [in press].

Since the end of the Cold War in 1989, the hostility of the Left towards human rights has waned: indeed in many instances it has been replaced by enthusiastic advocacy of the cause of human rights. This helps explain the fast growth of the subject that I mentioned at the start of this book. It is assumed by most advocates of human rights – from both the liberal and, increasingly, the socialist/post-socialist progressive camps – that the rights to which they have committed themselves need to be 'properly' entrenched so as to be able to control the vagaries of 'majoritarianism' (which is what elective democracies are increasingly called by those who argue for entrenched rights). Bills of rights that the judges cannot use to strike down laws are commonly thought by these scholars and activists to be useless, mere 'paper tigers', mockeries of the set of supra-political truths that have given rise to them. At the same time, human rights instruments have become more ambitious than in the past, moving beyond a Lockean preoccupation with property and liberty to embrace such modern concerns as privacy, free speech and (on occasion, usually in the hands of socialist-inclined academics) social and economic rights.

Why have so many on the radical side of politics now embraced this brand of supra-political human rights law? We glanced at this puzzle in chapter 1. The decline of socialist thinking, and the consequent drift of the Left to the centre ground, has narrowed the range of disputes that can these days arise between political actors and judicially interpreted rights-instruments. The judges in much of the democratic world seem less class-based than of old, more inclusive and modern in their interpretation of rights documents, less inclined to horrify the Left with extravagantly capitalist readings of allegedly basic rights. At a time when progressives have lost confidence in their ability to persuade voters to embrace social and economic reform, the attractions of a short-cut via judicially enforceable social and economic rights are obvious, and very difficult for many to resist. Nevertheless the idea that human rights law can enjoy authority as a force outside politics, able to impose its truth on politics in the name of human rights, remains as wrong now as it has been throughout the democratic era, and as wrong now as it was when judges regularly provided horrifying examples of their class bias. If not challenged, this misguided foundationalism retains the capacity both to debilitate the political process and seriously damage the legal system. I repeat: this is whether or not the human rights results in cases are outcomes of which we approve. We have to look to long-term structures, not to immediate but merely transient gains. The false promise of certainty offered by a supra-political reading of human rights by judges is a short-term fix, producing in its wake both a legalisation of politics and a politicisation of law. Both are damaging to our democratic culture.

The legalisation of politics

Martin Loughlin has described very well how good intentions can combine with fear to produce a flight from responsibility: 'Politicians in search of the median voter, having become fixated on their media images, lack the confidence to promote specific measures which protect the rights of unpopular minorities; enacting general principles enables responsibility for such action to pass from legislature to judiciary.'[30] The effect on the democratic process is stark. Where the political process is circumscribed by a strong and judicially enforceable bill of rights, discussion of a proposed law with a likely impact on human rights is transformed into a mere dress rehearsal for the definitive assessment, which will be legal in form and will follow rather than precede enactment. Cabinet ministers ask not, 'is this policy good for the country?' but rather 'can we get it past the lawyers?' In the legislative proceedings that follow, leading lawyers joust for supremacy via the elected representatives who intervene in debate to parrot their views. In some countries, as in Ireland, the senior judges can be drawn in by a process of reference, to give their overall ruling before the legislation is signed into law.[31] In other places, the United States for example, the public must wait to learn the fate of legislative initiatives in the litigation that can follow enactment at any point in time, and which has the potential to bring the whole statutory edifice tumbling to the ground.[32]

Even if judicial interventions like these were invariably wholly benign, there would still be something wrong about a system which turned the elective process into a mere overture for the real thing, a few pleasant tunes before the legal opera gets properly underway, with a bevy of highly paid tenors (very few sopranos) bellowing out their arias in

---

[30] M. Loughlin, 'Rights, Democracy and Law', in T. Campbell, K.D. Ewing and A. Tomkins (eds.), *Sceptical Essays on Human Rights* (Oxford University Press, Oxford, 2001), p. 53.

[31] See Article 26 of the Irish Constitution.

[32] The foundational case is *Marbury v Madison* 5 US (1 Cranch) 136 (1803). The power is not explicitly set out in the US Constitution.

a language few can understand – and with not a surtitle in sight for the now forgotten legislators sitting in the gods straining to follow what is happening to their laws. But the system is not benign, and this is not only (or even these days mainly) because judges are nasty and reactionary – on the whole (as I have already conceded) they are not. Much is often made of the extent to which the political process is dominated by money, but the same occurs to an even greater degree in the legal process, particularly in the power to launch litigation challenging the constitutionality of enacted law. Here money drives the system: it pays for the lawyers' opinions; covers the cost of taking the human rights law experts on threatening lobby missions to ministers; takes out the advertisements to deplore this or that initiative as an infringement of human rights; and then (if all else fails) underpins the litigation which forces government to defend afresh in the courts the law it (or a predecessor) has already persuaded the legislature to enact but which is now challenged as a 'breach of human rights'. The occasional *pro bono* case aside, these are not routes that are open to the poor, the disadvantaged, the voiceless for whom 'human rights' is supposed to be a specially tailored and supportive language. At its worst, the process of legal entrenchment takes these words from them and hands them to the rich, the powerful, the already fortunate, to do with what they will to consolidate their own advantage.

One of the most depressing effects that human rights jurisprudence has had on democracy has been the way in which a spurious commitment to freedom of expression has denied to legislatures the capacity properly to restrict the impact of money on the political process. Thus when in the immediate aftermath of the Watergate scandal, both the legislative and executive branches of the US federal government were energised to enact campaign funding controls, the good work done in levelling the political playing field was soon rent asunder by the US Supreme Court's highly particular reading of what the country's constitutional commitment to free speech actually entailed. In rejecting the imposition of spending limits on both candidates and third parties, the Court in *Buckley v Valeo*[33] ruled that 'the concept that government may restrict the speech of some elements of our society in order to enhance the relative voice of others is wholly foreign to the First Amendment.'[34] Other similar decisions soon followed, and the brief opening of a window that might have led to a properly democratised US system was closed – for decades at least and perhaps for ever. Even the generally more benign European system has been tempted into the same error, with a majority of the European Court of Human Rights having also felt themselves qualified to strike down British controls on election funding as a breach of the freedom of expression guarantee that is to be found in Article 10 of the European Convention on Human Rights, one that was not legitimised or excused as being 'necessary in a democratic society' (Article 10(2)).[35] One of the dissenting

[33] 424 US 1 (1976). K.D. Ewing, 'The Bill of Rights Debate: Democracy or Juristocracy in Britain', in K.D. Ewing, C.A. Gearty, and B.A. Hepple (eds.), *Human Rights and Labour Law* (Mansell, London, 1994), ch. 7 is excellent on this case and much else covered in this chapter.

[34] 424 US 1, at pp. 48–9.

[35] *Bowman v United Kingdom* (1998) 26 EHRR 1. See C.A. Gearty, 'Democracy and Human Rights in the European Court of Human Rights: A Critical Appraisal' 51 *Northern Ireland Law Quarterly Review* (2000) 381.

judges in the case, Judge Valticos, was surely right when he observed about the ruling that there was 'something slightly ridiculous in seeking to give the British Government lessons in how to hold elections and run a democracy'.[36] It is odd certainly that this bench of unelected lawyers should be more expert on what is 'necessary in a democratic society' than the elected representatives of the British people.

A particularly unfortunate consequence of the legalisation of what are effectively political decisions is that the dressing up of them in constitutional or 'human rights' form deprives the political community of the opportunity properly and critically to comment or engage with them. Once enunciated by the judges they become immutable law rather than mere opinion and as such are protected by the respect that the principle of separation of powers demands be shown towards the judiciary by the other two branches of the state. This is the case even where the ruling of the court itself appears to step outside its own remit. Of many examples that could be given, perhaps the most famous makes the point best of all. This was the US Supreme Court decision (in *Roe v Wade*[37]) that the country's bill of rights contains an implied right to terminate a pregnancy. The case has proved enduringly controversial, not least because it has seemed to take an issue of such central moral importance away from the elected representatives and place it firmly in the hands of an appointed community of inevitably unrepresentative lawyers, namely the federal judges. All that has flowed from *Roe v Wade* – the effort to add a 'pro-life' amendment to the

---

[36] (1998) 26 EHRR 1 at p. 22.   [37] 410 US 113 (1973).

US Constitution; the push for 'pro-life' justices on the Supreme Court; the development of a constitutional theory of originalism that was designed to lead eventually to the disowning of *Roe v Wade* (and may still do so) – has flowed from this central fact that the issue itself has been removed from what in a democracy is its proper place. Many years later the Justice who gave the lead opinion in *Roe*, Justice Harry Blackmun, told me in the course of an interview for the BBC that he had received some 75,000 letters on the case and that even then – eighteen years later – it was a 'rare day' that went by that he didn't 'have four, or five or six letters on the subject generally'.[38] I asked him about the effect of the decision on his life. He replied,

> Well (*chuckle*) shortly after the opinion came down, I had a speaking commitment out in Cedar Rapids, Iowa, and I encountered my first picketing which was a little strange and unusual for me. But that is not uncommon to this day, it depends where I go. If it is northern New Jersey, I am always picketed. Usually in my home state of Minnesota, I am picketed all . . . on my last two visits there. Los Angeles – always. Chicago – always. New York – never. And so it varies from place to place in the country. We did have a bullet come through the window of our apartment four years ago one night about 11.00pm. And over there is the tear from the chair in which the investigators found the bullet. So there has been some protection since that incident particularly. [39]

[38] C.A. Gearty, 'The Paradox of United States Democracy' 26 *University of Richmond Law Review* (1992) 259, at p. 262.   [39] *Ibid.*, 262–3.

There is something poignant about picketing in a democratic country which is designed to influence the opinion of persons exercising *de facto* political power but whose legal garb puts them beyond the reach of the ordinary voter.

The politicisation of law

If the effects on the political process are bad, the impact on the judicial branch can also be extremely negative. As the remarks by Mr Justice Blackmun that I have just quoted make clear, the central problem is that it is impossible to squeeze politics entirely out of a system of entrenched human rights law: it is a perpetuation of Lockean delusion to believe that these pre-political truths exist. Persevering with such folly merely causes the guardians of these impossible truths – the judiciary – to be infected with the very political virus from which they are supposed to be protecting the rest of their society. The effect of the decision in *Roe v Wade*, for example, is that the supposedly super-democratic United States is now a place where it is remarked without any intended irony that the most important task facing an elected president is his or her selection of members of the Supreme Court. I have already briefly alluded to the impact of the case on American public life. Of great importance here has been the Federalist Society, which since its formation in 1982 has worked to secure the appointment to the federal bench of judges sharing its conservative perspective on the world. It has been brilliantly successful: its first faculty advisor when it started in Chicago was Professor Antonin Scalia, now on the Supreme Court, and the Society counts among its most enthusiastic supporters the new Chief Justice John G. Roberts and the latest appointment to the Court, Samuel A. Alito Jr. None of this has happened by accident: rather it has been the result of hard political graft. The rewards of such success include special access to the Bush White House and guest speeches at the Society's annual dinners by such confidantes of the current president as Karl Rove. Speaking to the Society in November 2005, Rove described the Senate's confirmation of some 200 of Mr Bush's judicial nominees as among the President's greatest achievements, bringing about change in 'our courts and our legal culture', something that 'would not have been possible were it not for the Federalist Society'. Rove joked that the group had so 'thoroughly infiltrated the White House' that the President's Chief of Staff had asked him to announce a staff meeting after the dinner at which he was speaking.[40]

We should beware of seeing the squabbles over the likes of Samuel Alito, Harriet Miers, Clarence Thomas and before these three (and bitterest of all) Robert Bork[41] as quintessentially American and therefore easy to discount. Less high-octane but nevertheless intensely charged debate on the composition of the judicial branch has become part and parcel of democratic culture in most of those societies that have asked the judges to define and guard human-rights-based truth on their behalf. There was quite a political rumpus over the appointment of the United Kingdom's current judge on the

---

[40] See 'Rove Addresses Federalist Society' *Washington Post* 11 November 2005.

[41] On which see R.H. Bork, *The Tempting of America. The Political Seduction of the Law* (Sinclair-Stevenson, London, 1990), esp. chs. 14–18.

European Court of Human Rights, Sir Nicholas Bratza, with critics complaining (somewhat unfairly it has to be said) about his involvement as an advocate for the government in cases thought hostile to civil liberties which had been brought by the Thatcher administration during the 1980s. Even Britain's (in this context) very timid Human Rights Act has thrown a spotlight on the collection of South African, Scottish and Irish men, with the occasional Englishman and very occasional woman, who keep an eye on the human rights behaviour of our democratic representatives, like teachers in a school playground. It is perfectly natural and right that the public should want to know more about their teachers, and – as the UK prime minister Tony Blair reportedly suggested in relation to teachers proper recently – arrange to have them sacked if they don't like what they are doing. Perhaps we are not as far away as we might want to believe from such a proposal in law, what the Americans call 'recall'?

A further risk in seeking to accommodate the inevitable political dimension to the task of judging, a dimension that as I have said cannot be squeezed out by calling the issues under scrutiny human rights law, is that the judicial branch comes increasingly to ape the political. Thus we have seen the emergence of Grand Chambers in the European Court of Human Rights[42] and expanded panels of judges sitting on cases in the House of Lords, an implicit recognition of the democratic insight that 'the wisdom of the crowd' might be a better route to truth than the logic of legal argument. The

[42] Convention for the Protection of Human Rights and Fundamental Freedoms (as amended) Article 43.

latter development in the Lords is relatively recent and has undoubtedly added weight to recent lords' rulings on controversial issues like torture[43] and detention without trial.[44] With the expansion of the Council of Europe, cases before the European Court of Human Rights are no longer heard by judges drawn from all the Member States as was the case in the past. However with issues considered exceptionally important, a much larger gathering of such eminent figures (many more than the usual seven) is convened. These jurists then seek to divine the legal truth on an issue in a way that seems, however, to be quintessentially political – by a show of hands. And just like parliamentarians – but unlike supposed Truth-finders – in reaching its decisions the Court does not feel duty bound to follow its past decisions. It may depart from these in the light of present day conditions or the situation on the ground in the Member States. The effect of this can be seen in, for example, the Court's interpretation of the extent to which the Convention accords rights to transsexuals. Of course the document, drafted shortly after the end of the Second World War, makes no reference to such personages. But equally the guarantees of respect for privacy (Article 8) and of the right to marry (Article 12) can be extended without too much difficulty to such special cases. In the first case on the issue in 1986,[45] the vote had been twelve to three against on Article 8 and a unanimous negative on Article 12. In the next decision, in 1990, the majorities against the applicant had shrunk to ten to eight and

[43] *A and others v Secretary of State for the Home Department (No. 2)* [2005] UKHL 71.

[44] *A and others v Secretary of State for the Home Department* [2004] UKHL 56.   [45] *Rees v United Kingdom* (1986) 9 EHRR 56.

fourteen to four respectively.[46] Eight years later it was eleven to nine against on Article 8 but back at eighteen to two on Article 12.[47] In 2002 came the breakthrough case, *Goodwin v United Kingdom*, a unanimous ruling that both articles had in fact been infringed by a failure to recognise the applicant's transsexuality. It seemed that 'the fair balance that is inherent in the Convention now tilt[ed] decisively in favour of the applicant.'[48] But how could this be known by any process other than a political one, albeit carefully camouflaged in human rights clothes?

This trend in human rights litigation does not go unnoticed by those who seek to influence political outcomes. The Federalist Society takes the direct route of trying to shape the composition of the bench. Closer to home, lobbying groups are more modest in their goals. Non-parties to cases increasingly seek, by filing amicus briefs, to influence the outcome of litigation in which technically they ought to have no interest: judges allow this because they know in their hearts that they are involved in a kind of law-making, albeit one disguised as Truth-finding.[49] The same momentum has led to more and more third party interventions with barristers now routinely making submissions in our senior courts on behalf of clients who have no specific engagement in the case. The United States Supreme Court has been familiar with such briefs for decades; the *Padilla* case currently before that body –

[46] *Cossey v United Kingdom* (1990) 13 EHRR 622.
[47] *Sheffield and Horsham v United Kingdom* (1998) 27 EHRR 163.
[48] (2002) 35 EHRR 447, para. 93.
[49] See S. Hannett, 'Third Party Interventions: In the Public Interest?' [2003] *Public Law* 128. See R. Smith, 'Test Case Strategies and the Human Rights Act' 1 *Justice Journal* (2004) 65.

on executive detention in the context of the executive's self-declared 'war on terror' – has stimulated an *amicus brief* on UK and Israeli law from no fewer than fifteen academics and practitioners from around the world.[50] Drives to make the judiciary more representative and accountable likewise draw their strength from recognition that what judges do is, in these days of human rights litigation, more overtly political than in the past.[51] This is all well and good, inevitable given the legalisation of human rights that I have been discussing, but might we wake up one day to find that the strengths that the idea of the rule of law brought to our culture have been fatally compromised by these human-rights-inspired concessions to the political? Already the British government in general, and the Prime Minister in particular, have difficulty in seeing the rule of law as something different from the other 'vested interests' which they feel they have to take on and destroy for the good of the public.

A solution?

So far I have painted quite a negative picture of the impact of human rights on the discourse of law, describing an effect that I have argued is damaging both to human rights and to law. I said earlier that I would suggest a solution to the problems I have identified and now is the time to do so. It would be tempting to say that the best legal avenue of all is one planted

---

[50] The case is *Padilla v C T Hanft*, not yet decided.

[51] See 'Lord Chancellor Calls for More Public Involvement in Appointing Judges' *Guardian* 23 January 2006, p. 15.

only with positive rights, a route to just outcomes in individual cases in which there are to be found no generalised human rights at all. It is, I think, too late for such a call as this to have any chance of being heard. The language of human rights is here to stay and as I pointed out earlier it undoubtedly does valuable work in certain spheres. To remove it altogether would be unavoidably to seem to be making a strong negative statement about human rights in general, and this is not something that our liberal culture can afford to do. The grip of decency on public affairs is too precarious for us to let go of this language in the legal as much as in the political field: this is a point I developed at length in chapter 2.

The issue is not one of the language as such but one of authority: how can we hold on to a law of human rights which does useful civilising work but at the same time does not succumb to the temptation to lord it over politics? The international human rights model might be thought by some to be the answer, but here the crisis is one not of over- but of under-enforceability: standing outside politics, the inability of this branch of international law to make itself felt on the ground is sometimes so complete that one is left wondering why it is called law at all. The constitutional bills of rights in Germany, Japan, the United States, Ireland and South Africa provide paradigm examples of the kind of separation between politics and law that I have been attacking in this chapter. There is something inherently distasteful about elected representatives waiting to see whether their judgments about the public interest, made on a bona fide basis with the interests of the community genuinely at heart, meet with the approval of a bench of unelected and unaccountable lawyers. Canada is a bit better in this regard, since its Supreme Court can have its verdicts on human (or in this context 'charter') rights overturned by the legislature as long as the elected representatives make it crystal clear that this is what they are doing – by inserting a so-called 'notwithstanding' clause into their parliamentary bills.[52] However this happens so rarely as to be almost useless as a political counterweight to the courts' version of right and wrong: the pressure not to defy judicial versions of rights has proved next to impossible to resist. The New Zealand equivalent on the other hand, allowing rights-based oversight of administrative powers but restricting the judicial power vis-à-vis legislation to one of mere interpretation, is so grudging and minimalist in its use of the language of rights that the good work that rights-talk can usually be relied on to do is greatly restricted. Under this New Zealand model, all the judges can do is fiddle with the words of any given law so as to magic a rights-consistent meaning out of them if they can, but if this proves impossible because the words are clear, then the judges have no further role to play.[53]

The answer to our question is much closer to home. It is the UK Human Rights Act. Here we have a set of clear human rights, with duties imposed on courts and public authorities to make sure that these rights are properly protected and enforced. Drawn from the European Convention on Human Rights, these rights are concerned with the avoidance of cruelty (the guarantee of the right to life; the abolition of the death penalty; the prohibition on torture, inhuman and

---

[52] Canadian Charter of Rights and Freedoms, s. 33.
[53] New Zealand Bill of Rights Act 1990, ss. 4–6.

degrading treatment and punishment; the ban on slavery, forced labour and servitude) and with enabling individuals to thrive both individually and in community with others (the right to respect for privacy; the freedoms of thought, conscience and religion; the right to marry; the prohibition on discrimination; the (qualified) right to property; and the right to education). The Act contains civil rights such as: the right to liberty; the right to fair procedures in the criminal and civil spheres; and a guarantee of no punishment without law. There are also to be found various democratic rights such as the guarantee of free elections and the freedoms of expression, assembly and association. All public authorities are required to act compatibly with these rights, and – following the New Zealand model – the courts are empowered to interpret all legislation in a way that is consistent with these Convention rights '[s]o far as it is possible to do so'.[54] Various remedies, including damages, are provided where public authorities are found to have strayed into forbidden, rights-abusing territory.[55]

Looked at from outside, and presented in the way I have just presented them, these rights do look like a set of truths above the political process which are being imposed by the judges over the heads of elected representatives. This appearance is deceptive. The first point to make is that the European Convention itself contains many exceptions to most of its own rights, and these qualifications are carried through into the Human Rights Act. There is no room for Bentham-like chiding about the nonsense of the absolute claims in this

---

[54] Human Rights Act 1998, s. 3(1).   [55] Human Rights Act 1998, ss. 7–9.

charter: only a few very basic guarantees such as on torture and slavery come with no caveats whatsoever, and presumably not even Bentham would have disapproved of this. Secondly, the Convention also provides its own self-destruct button, in the form of a power on the part of States to derogate from the bulk of its provisions where this is judged to be necessary on account of a 'war or other public emergency threatening the life of the nation'.[56] This override clause has also been carried into the British law. But the genius of the Human Rights Act lies in a third way in which it deliberately undermines its own authority, inviting the political back in to control the legal at just the moment when the supremacy of the legal discourse seems assured. There are two points to make here. First, unlike the kinds of constitutional bills of rights that are to be found in the United States, India, South Africa, Germany, Ireland and so on – in fact most places where such rights have been introduced – the UK Human Rights Act carries within its substance no protection against later repeal by simple majority. It has not been inoculated against subsequent political attack. So when in Autumn 2005 the then front runner for the Conservative Party leadership David Davis set out a personal manifesto for office oozing with hostility for human rights, this was a position from which the judges would have been unable to protect the country. In fact politics proved up to the task, with Davis failing in his leadership bid, being beaten by a younger opponent whose attitude to our subject seems altogether more friendly. It is important – and good for the long-term health of

[56] Convention for the Protection of Human Rights and Fundamental Freedoms, Article 15.

the human rights culture of this country – that such a frontal assault on the subject should have been possible (and better still that it was seen-off so quickly).

Secondly, and equally importantly, the Human Rights Act denies the courts the capacity to strike down parliamentary legislation for incompatibility with the rights set out in the Act. The orthodox precedents have not been followed, not even the modestly equipped Canadian Charter with its inbuilt allowing of retaliatory legislative action in the form of bills with 'notwithstanding charter rights' clauses. But nor has the Human Rights Act gone down the somewhat anaemic New Zealand route. Instead the higher courts may issue declarations of incompatibility, and both Parliament and the executive must consider what to do about these, and in particular whether the law should be brought into line with what the courts have declared to be the requirements of human rights.[57] Crucially however, this is all that the non-judicial branches of the State are required to do: think twice, not blindly obey. These declarations of incompatibility are courteous requests for a conversation, not pronouncements of truth from on high. At the time of writing there have been some twelve such declarations that have survived scrutiny in appeal proceedings. The famous decision by the House of Lords in December 2004 was one of these.[58] In that case, the system of detention of suspected international terrorists introduced after 11 September 2001 was found to have infringed the guarantee against unjustified discrimination in Article 14 of the Convention but

---

[57] Human Rights Act 1998, ss. 4 and 10; sched 2.
[58] *A v Secretary of State for the Home Department*, n. 44 above.

this did not lead to the setting aside of the law, in other words to the immediate release of those who were being held by dint of these provisions. Rather the executive and the legislative branches had to decide whether or not to act, which they duly did, introducing and putting into effect new law (the Prevention of Terrorism Act 2005) which was not open to the same human rights objections as that which it was now superseding. I shall return to this case and its aftermath in chapter 4 – but for now we should note how human rights worked both as law and as a stimulus to a political rethink. The same is true of House of Lords decisions on life sentences for convicted murderers[59] and on the rights of post-operative transsexuals:[60] the judges have not liked these laws, have found in the language of human rights a ready way of articulating their distaste but have not turned their point-of-view into one which has deprived Parliament of the law-making and law-unmaking powers that are its by (democratic) right.

This very careful construction of the Human Rights Act both asserts human rights to be important and at the same time allows judicial versions of them to be over-ridden by Parliament. In other words it reflects the human rights mask that the United Kingdom has chosen to wear. Those of us who believe in human rights all hope that it stays put and argue that it should. We believe that donning this legal mask has made us a better society, one in which there is a chance of less cruelty and a greater set of opportunities for people to flourish in their

---

[59] *R (Anderson) v Secretary of State for the Home Department* [2002] UKHL 46, [2003] 1 AC 837.
[60] *Bellinger v Bellinger* [2003] UKHL 21, [2003] 2 AC 467.

lives.[61] I think the record of the Human Rights Act so far in these regards is not bad at all on the whole. But this human rights mask does not necessarily reflect any deep supra-political truths. It can be torn away should the British people through their elected representatives so decide. This might be because the judges have simply got wrong what human rights requires, with their mistake then needing to be rectified, or it might be because Parliament has decided to dispense with rights altogether. It is our job, and the job of all those who care about human rights, to make sure that this second eventuality, this terrible unmasking, never occurs, though the first might and we should not be afraid of it when it does. All this requires us to talk, to persuade, to argue, to fight the political fight, and not to rely on judicial guardians to protect us from the crowd. That is exactly as it should be: defenders of human rights in the United Kingdom have a great story, what they need to do is sell it to the general public, not rely on judges to impose silence in the name of a truth that falsely claims to be above politics.

---

[61] Cf. J. Webber, 'A Modest (but Robust) Defence of Statutory Bills of Rights', in T. Campbell, J. Goldsworthy and A. Stone (eds.), *Human Rights without a Bill of Rights: Institutional Performance and Reform in Australia* (Ashgate, London, 2006 [in press]).

4

The crisis of national security

The following sequence of events may have a familiar ring.[1] A terrorist attack takes place in central London. Six people are killed and some forty injured. The Prime Minister, having already banned all political demonstrations in London, now proposes the repeal of habeas corpus. The Metropolitan Police Commissioner gives an interview in the media in which he declares that there are 10,000 armed terrorists at large in London. An extra 50,000 special constables are sworn in to save the city. Teams of police oversee special workers, scouring the sewers for terrorist explosives. The Queen herself intervenes, observing that she was beginning to wish that all these terrorists would 'be lynch-lawed on the spot'. A leading public intellectual observes that '[t]he London masses, who have shown great sympathy towards [the terrorists' cause] will be made wild and driven into the arms of a reactionary government' as a result of the attack. But much later the atrocity is credited with having turned the thoughts of a future prime minister towards dealing not just with the terrorism but with its political causes as well.

These events are true, but drawn not from this century, not even from the last, but rather from 1867. The prime minister is Benjamin Disraeli not Tony Blair; the metropolitan police commissioner Richard Mayne rather than Sir Ian Blair or

[1] What follows is drawn from G. Bennett, 'Legislative Responses to Terrorism: A View from Britain' 109 *Penn State Law Review* (2005) 947.

Sir John Stevens; the Queen is Victoria not Elizabeth the Second; the public intellectual is Karl Marx not Noam Chomsky; and the future PM is of course Gladstone rather than Gordon Brown (or David Cameron). The terrorists were the Irish Fenians, the Al Qaeda of their day. Their totemic status as the bogeymen of British society was enjoyed for far longer than Osama Bin Laden and his cohorts are likely to be able to manage, though the state's reaction to both is hauntingly similar. Here is the Home Secretary Sir Samuel Hoare, explaining that new anti terrorism legislation rushed through in a week in August 1939 was necessitated by a 'very remarkable document' which had been uncovered by the police, the 'S Plan', which – he said – indicated that the IRA was intent on attacking the water supply, the drainage system, the transport infrastructure and the electricity supply, and – as though this were not enough – that the organisation was even 'engaged upon a plan to blow up the Houses of Parliament'.[2] Nobody paid much attention to the fact that the government had had, on its own quiet admission, possession of this terrifying document for seven months, so why act on it only now, with the Summer recess days away and everything having to be done in a hectic rush? Perhaps the urgency was required by the fact that, as the Home Secretary reported to the House of Commons, the authorities were aware that the IRA campaign was 'being closely watched and actively stimulated by foreign organisations'. In that Summer, the Summer of 1939, people naturally thought of the Nazis and Mussolini, but nobody could

---

[2] K.D. Ewing and C.A. Gearty, *The Struggle for Civil Liberties* (Oxford University Press, Oxford, 2000) ch. 8 has the details. For a very good account see O.G. Lomas, 'The Executive and the Anti-Terrorist Legislation of 1939' [1980] *Public Law* 16.

be quite sure because Sir Samuel asked members 'not to press me for details'. Years later, it turned out it was the Irish-Americans he had in mind.

Or, much closer to the present day, take 1996, when new terrorism laws were rushed through by the then Home Secretary Michael Howard on the basis of a supposedly imminent IRA campaign to celebrate the eightieth anniversary of the Easter rising. There was the usual panoply of confidential briefings, laws passed in a day, the peers kept at it for hours to save the nation, the Queen waiting by her bedside, pen at hand. But the 'campaign' wasn't due (if it was due at all) when the government said it was, Easter being a movable rather than a fixed feast day: the government were being urgent in the wrong week. Or remember 1998 when the emergency parliamentary response to the Omagh bombings included such logically unrelated initiatives as a new offence of conspiracy to commit terrorist attacks abroad. The Terrorism Act 2000, now the key statute in the United Kingdom's framework of anti-terrorism laws, was only passed because the problem of Irish-based subversive violence was coming to an end. The response to this that would have been obvious to a previous generation of politicians, those like Roy Jenkins who had so reluctantly introduced these measures in the first place, would have been to repeal the legislation entirely, holding a day of civil libertarian celebration to mark the event. Instead, the outgoing Conservative administration of John Major commissioned an independent report to review these laws which *required* the reviewer to assume their necessity.[3] The incoming Labour government headed by

---

[3] *Inquiry into Legislation Against Terrorism* (1996, Cm. 3420, Chair: Lord Lloyd of Berwick).

Tony Blair promptly legislated on the basis of this report, despite the Party's decades-long opposition to terrorism laws. Matters then reverted to type, with the supersession of the IRA by Al Qaeda fuelling the anti-terrorism laws of 2001, 2005 and (very soon no doubt) 2006. The kinds of things terrorism laws do are no longer embarrassing and compromising and to be endured for only so long as they are absolutely necessary – rather they are becoming essential saviours of our society, safeguards against an otherwise inevitable barbarism: in short the new common sense of our age.

Challenging human rights

If we ask the question, as the title to this book does, 'Can Human Rights Survive?', then we must admit that an optimistic answer is least obvious in this field of national security, which these days invariably means counter-terrorism. In the ethical grammar that underlies our way of describing the world, danger and fear are fast replacing dignity and hope as the terms that come first to mind when we describe the shape of the world in which we live. In chapters 2 and 3, I identified the core idea behind human rights as being the equality of esteem in which we are all held in virtue of our humanity. This unfolds into a respect for dignity which demands both an end to cruelty and humiliation on the one hand and a commitment to human flourishing on the other: these were the themes in particular of chapter 2. In chapter 3 I looked at how the idea of human rights can be made to work better than it presently does, to thrive as well as merely to survive, by being connected in an effective and non-contradictory way with two of the other large ethical ideas of our contemporary age: the rule of law and democracy. Terrorism laws challenge both the core proposition underpinning human rights and each of its three manifestations. In place of equality of esteem they offer, very particularly, inequality of esteem, judging people not by the fact that they simply are but by where they are from and by which culture or faith it is to which they belong. We have been referring to the United Kingdom and it is a good case-study through which to make the general point. Recently we have had legislation passed by a Parliament of elected representatives which, quite specifically, provided for the indefinite detention without trial of non-national as opposed to national suspected 'terrorists'[4] and did so in explicit defiance of human rights.[5] When this deliberate discrimination was declared incompatible with the European Convention on Human Rights, the same House of Commons (with the Lords and Her Majesty of course) then responded with, among other initiatives, house arrest. This is a form of coercion that until enactment of the 2005 Prevention of Terrorism Act was surely thought incapable of being used in a modern democratic state, much less one publicly devoted *at the same time* to establishing a human rights culture. (The statute avoids the actual term 'house arrest' but this is what its words amount to.)

The rule of law is also challenged by terrorism legislation. If we stay with the UK, we find wide administrative discretions given to the police to stop and search without reasonable suspicion and to detain without charge for (as first

---

4 Anti-terrorism, Crime and Security Act 2001.
5 See Joint Committee on Human Rights (JCHR), Second Report, *Anti-terrorism, Crime and Security Bill* HL (2001–2002) 37, HC (2001–2002) 372; JCHR, Fifth Report, *Anti-terrorism, Crime and Security Bill: Further Report* HL (2001–2002) 51, HC (2001–2002) 420.

proposed in the Terrorism Bill 2005) as long as three months (even twenty-eight days remains an unconscionably long time). Noteworthy as well are the new wide and vague crimes that are to be found in the standard anti-terrorism laws and the truncated legal procedures – the special courts, the restricted rules of evidence, the security-vetted judges and the like. There is also the extensive undermining of political speech that has to be taken into account: the over-broad definition of terrorism in the 2000 Act which can easily embrace direct action groups on the margins of our political discourse;[6] the application of terrorism law extra-jurisdictionally so that it can be used against those who are seeking to overthrow tyranny and dictatorship abroad;[7] the expansion in the use of proscription powers which now makes it normal for political associations within a jurisdiction to be banned on suspicion of involvement in terrorism;[8] the chilling effect on speech of the stop and search powers in terrorism law which start out as protections against Al Qaeda and end up as devices to stop protesters from going to arms fairs[9] and to sustain the expulsion of old men from party meetings for heckling the Foreign Secretary.[10] All these powers are already in place in the UK, and yet more flows off the government presses: the Terrorism Bill currently before Parliament proposes a set of new offences such as that of glorifying 'the commission or preparation (whether in the past, in the future or generally)' of acts of terrorism. We all know who is likely to be

---

[6] Terrorism Act 2000 s. 1.   [7] *Ibid.* esp. ss. 1(4) and 59–61.

[8] *Ibid.* Part II; Terrorism Bill 2005 cls. 21 and 22.

[9] *R (Gillan) v Metropolitan Police Commissioner* [2006] UKHL 12.

[10] Walter Wolfgang: see *Guardian* 29 September 2005.

caught by this particularly egregious crime, and it won't be the Queen reminiscing fondly about the activities of William of Orange (as he then was). Nor will it be admirers of Oliver Cromwell or even, these days, the Camden Irish Club gathering to celebrate Easter 1916. At least the terrorism laws of the 1970s and 1980s had the decency to be explicit about the fact that they were after only the Irish.

The sad thing is that the UK is just one example among many that could be cited; it is part of the mainstream, not an illiberal exception.[11] The affront to democracy posed by terrorism laws goes deeper than the mere undermining of political speech, serious though this undoubtedly is. There is also the structural abuse of perpetually rushed legislation, with there always being said to be only just a couple of days before all terrorist hell breaks loose unless this or that legislature buckles before the will of the executive. Again this is a general point for which the UK – with its long record of anti-terrorism law – stands as a dismal exemplar. It is demeaning to see successive UK parliaments over many generations trapped between the politics of the last atrocity – demanding that a recent attack be met with a strong anti-terrorist response – and the politics of the next atrocity – which insist on draconian laws now to prevent the horrors that lie in the future.[12] In such a frenetic political climate, one that we have seen the British prime

---

[11] Later in this chapter I will turn to the United States where the attack on human rights has been altogether more severe.

[12] For the historical background see C.A. Gearty, 'Political Violence and Civil Liberties', in C. McCrudden and G. Chambers (eds.), *Individual Rights and the Law in Britain* (The Law Society and Clarendon Press, Oxford, 1994) ch. 5, esp. pp. 162–8.

minister and certain of his colleagues embrace in recent years and especially since the 7 July 2005 attacks in London, normal politics have become very difficult. As Mr Blair has frankly admitted, the police tell him what they want and his job is to go and get it. We should be grateful for the small mercy that the police service has within its culture a still discernible civil libertarian conscience which acts as a restraint on their own requests: that modifying hand is not likely to be found at no. 10 Downing Street to any great extent, at least while its current incumbent is in office. It is not the terrorists who are changing the rules, it is this government, and one moreover that does not even have the excuse of being bombed, as Mrs Thatcher was in Brighton, or attacked with mortars as Mr Major's cabinet was in Downing Street. If the rules could survive these kinds of crises in the past, why is it that they are so inadequate now? Suicide bombers are new and dangerous of course, but in their time so were dynamite, Semtex and remote-controlled explosions: a fear-driven society will always find something unique, and unprecedented about the latest way that its members might be killed.

Where do human rights fit in this dismal story? Anxiety about terrorism has gripped the public discourse at exactly the same time as our subject has at last been securing centre-stage. The two are strong rivals for the same public space. In past outbreaks of executive-induced hysteria in Britain, those of 1867 and 1939 for example, there were no human rights around for the authorities to have to consider. Even in 1974 and 1996, the human rights element to the British political equation was a distant one, to be found in Strasbourg rather than in the law courts on the Strand. But the present UK government which I have just been criticising is the very same administration which in 1998 enacted the Human Rights Act and which is even today working hard to establish an Equality and Human Rights Commission. How have such draconian attacks on the basic DNA of human rights – dignity, legality and democracy – been able to take place in a society presided over by a human-rights-respecting administration, one which requires of its public authorities that they adhere to the extensive range of political, civil and some social and economic rights that are to be found in the European Convention on Human Rights and Fundamental Freedoms? Or to switch from one side of the Atlantic to the other, how can a country which as we have seen in chapter 2 has been a major driving force behind the growth of human rights in the post-1945 world, the United States, now think it permissible explicitly to disregard all that our subject stands for in its self-declared 'war on terror'? And where the United Kingdom and the United States go, other countries willingly follow: in the field of counter-terrorism and human rights, these two secure, stable democracies make the weather, creating the climate in which human rights activists the world over must work. In the way that these states conduct themselves vis-à-vis human rights, they matter out of all proportion to their sovereign space.

Of course it is the case that these terrorism laws are criticised by many. But not everybody outside government shares this view. In this chapter we directly confront the mystery of how it is that human-rights-loving people – intellectuals, academics and judges as well as democratic politicians – can at the same time create, defend and support the kind of repressive laws I have just been attacking. The problem is at one level about an explicit conflict between counter-terrorism laws and human rights. But it is also about something more ominous altogether: a supposed lack of conflict between the two, flowing from a redefinition of human rights the effect of which is to excuse repression as necessary to prevent the destruction of human rights values. On this analysis, and it is a depressingly widespread though not as yet universal one, messing about aggressively with people, suspending the ordinary processes of law, narrowing the civic space so as to exclude alternative points of view all turn out to be okay from a human rights perspective: not a bad result if you are a dedicated counter-terrorist, less easy to explain if your public posture is as a human rights defender. Flowing out of this critique, in the last part of the chapter, I will show that this dangerous embrace between counter-terrorism laws and human rights is not inevitable, and that there are ways in which human rights principles can fight back, setting their own agenda and not lapsing into an exaggerated anxiety that offers carte blanche to the security perspective. As we shall see there are strong signs in many democracies, not least the United Kingdom and the United States, of just such a fight-back having commenced, so the chapter will not need to end on an entirely pessimistic note.

But what about the nature of the threat posed by terrorism? Have I not so far grossly underestimated it and therefore ignored the need for dramatic action to prevent its damaging effects, action which may be required even if what it involves is grossly unattractive from a human rights point of view? Before we turn either to the human rights problems I have just outlined or how to address them, there is an important, preliminary set of questions to consider. What is terrorism? Why is it said to be so different from ordinary (albeit serious) crime, warranting extreme state actions that would not otherwise be thought for one moment to be justified? How did the subject of terrorism come to be so central to our political discourse? Why has the counter-terrorism perspective thrived in the way that it has, driven forward so many laws in so many countries around the world, subverted so much of what we assume the ideas of democracy, human rights and the rule of law are there to defend? Where does this idea of terrorism come from? What meaning does the word take on today, and why has it proved so powerful that it now threatens the integrity of the entire human rights project? As we shall see, it is quite wrong to view the events of 11 September 2001 as pivotal in this respect. The answers lie deeper in history than this and far away from New York and Washington, in that part of the world currently uneasily shared – and on grossly unequal terms – between the state of Israel on the one hand and the Palestinian people on the other.

Terror and terrorism

For many years I worried with all the other so-called 'terrorism experts' about the fact that there was no proper, objective definition of terrorism. I even abandoned a law text-book I planned on the subject on account of the inadequacy of my introductory chapter. In the end I wrote a book on terrorism that was more about language and the power of labels than it was about killing and kidnapping.[13] This was because it had eventually dawned on me that the whole point of the subject of terrorism was that there was no definition. The importance of

---

[13] C.A. Gearty, *Terror* (Faber and Faber, London, 1991).

the subject, its utility to those who mattered, relied upon the impossibility of it ever being tied down. For the moment terrorism is given an objective meaning, one that can be commonly agreed, is a dangerous moment for the experts, a point in time when the term risks taking on a rational life of its own, and therefore being rendered capable of being ascribed to events beyond the experts' power of categorisation.[14] Take just as an example a straightforward definition, one that sees as terrorist violence, the intentional or reckless killing or injuring of non-combatants, or the doing of severe damage to their property, in order to communicate a political message. Expressed like this, it is clear that terrorism is a method of violence, and as such is one that can be used by any actor who has chosen to deploy violence in pursuit of this or that political goal. It can, it is true, be used by the kind of weak group that has few other military or political options in its locker: the Al Qaedas and ETAs of this world. But it can equally well be deployed as a method of violence by other, stronger forces, by guerrilla organisations for example that are able to muster other kinds of military action as well if the need arises, and by insurgent forces in a civil war situation where terror violence may be just one option among many. In failed states it is available, among other brutal techniques, to all the ambitious, power-hungry factions.

It is equally clearly a kind of political violence that can be deployed by state forces, either in isolation – the French action in sinking Greenpeace's *Rainbow Warrior* in 1985 is a good example as might be the American decision to bomb

---

[14] For an elaboration on what follows see C.A. Gearty, 'Terrorism and Morality' [2003] *European Human Rights Law Review* 377.

Tripoli in 1986; or in tandem with other kinds of violence in the context of a serious armed conflict – examples that come to mind would be the allied bombing of Dresden and other German cities towards the end of World War II and the nuclear attacks on Hiroshima and Nagasaki in 1945. Describing terrorism as a kind of political violence in this way is not necessarily to say that it is wrong, just as to call something an aerial bombardment or an invasion or a siege is not to condemn it. The question of morality is separate from the issue of attribution. On this account to call this or that action terrorist is to prepare the ground for a discussion of its legitimacy – it sets up rather than answers that important question.

Now of course this is not at all how we use the term today. First and most importantly we have come to view terrorism not as a method of violence but rather as a category of person, a kind of militant rather than a kind of tactic, the sort of thing a person is rather than the kind of thing a person does. So we have terrorist organisations, terrorist groups, terrorist leaders and so on, and these labels do not require evidence of specific actions in order to be made to stick, to secure coherence in our discourse. Once a group is classified as terrorist it becomes terrorist to all intents and purposes – the label does not depend on specific acts of terror to be made to work. Second, as indicated earlier with regard to UK law, legal definitions of terrorism are invariably much wider than the core meaning I have just given to the term.[15] In most systems of

---

[15] The Terrorism Act 2000, s. 1 is a good case in point. See also the draft UN Comprehensive Convention on International Terrorism as recommended by the Ad Hoc Committee on Terrorism: GA Official Records, 57th Session, Supplement No. 37 (A/57/37) 11 February 2002.

laws the notion of terrorism characteristically reaches beyond assaults on civilians to incorporate violence against property and attacks on a country's infrastructure. Indeed some legal accounts of terrorism are so broad that they incorporate direct action and extreme forms of civil disobedience.[16] Once a group is labelled terrorist by reference to one or other of this wide set of criteria, it is then terrorist, not only (as I earlier said) *regardless* of what it does but also sometimes *in spite of* what it does. A group might be terrorist without ever having lifted a finger in anger against anybody whatsoever. It might still be terrorist even when it is involved in specifically non-violent actions. Thus, as has happened recently in Palestine, a political party engaged in electoral politics (indeed winning an election) can nevertheless be regarded as terrorist and therefore as beyond the pale of proper political discourse. That 'therefore' is important. For thirdly, we have completely lost sight of the fact that political terror is a description of a kind of violence and not necessarily a moral condemnation of that violence. To contemporary ears, to call something terrorist is at the same time to condemn it as morally wrong: the value judgment is packed into the description, the 'is' has been elided into the 'ought' or more accurately in this case the 'ought not'. Fourthly and finally to complete this story of verbal degradation, we have so contrived matters that terrorism is now widely thought of as something of which state authorities – acting either directly or through authorised paramilitary forces – are incapable. Even if what the state does is both violent and designed to spread terror

---

[16] See for a good survey B. Golder and G. Williams, 'What is "Terrorism"? Problems of Legal Definition' 27 *University of New South Wales Law Journal* (2004) 270.

among its own people – a sadly not uncommon occurrence as is obvious from a perusal of the recent annual reports from Amnesty[17] and Human Rights Watch[18] – it nevertheless cannot be described as terror or terrorist action because those terms have now come to be invariably applied to sub-state actors. Even worse, this kind of terror by the state might find itself with luck and a bit of careful spin being reclassified as counter-terrorism, in other words as inherently good in the same way that terrorism is inherently bad.

The evolution of the term terrorism from a description of a kind of violence to a morally loaded condemnation of the actions of subversive groups regardless of the context of their actions or even sometimes their non-violent nature should not surprise us. It is a movement in language that operates wholly in favour of state authorities, taking their conduct out of the realm of terror, however horrible, while at the same time giving them a capacity to dump this powerfully opprobrious label on their political opponents. No wonder authoritarian leaders everywhere, the Mugabes and Burmese juntas of this world, are such counter-terrorist enthusiasts. None of this explains, however, a further twist in deployment of the language of terrorism, one that has great and direct relevance today, not least to our subject of human rights. This is the way in which the term has shed any kind of locational exactitude and become a manifestation of a universal crisis, a violent version of the plague, something that crosses

---

[17] Amnesty International Report 2005, *The State of the World's Human Rights* (London, 2005).

[18] Human Rights Watch, *World Report 2006* (Human Rights Watch and Seven Stories Press, New York, 2006).

boundaries at will, swooping upon unsuspecting peoples out of the blue and bringing destruction and death in its wake. In its contemporary form terrorism is no longer a particular kind of violence that this or that gang or group in this or that country do; rather it is said to be part of a pattern of systematic international violence against which a 'global war on terror' now needs to be waged. This idea of a world-wide contagion of terror inspired by evil forces with designs on western civilisation – so commonly spoken of today as something new and unprecedented and uniquely terrifying – in fact originates well before 11 September 2001. Exploring its origins takes us back to the very beginnings of the modern distortion of our subject, the late 1960s.

This is where Palestine and Israel come in. Until 1968, descriptions of post World War II sub-state political violence were largely informed by an anti-colonial narrative, one that saw the use of such force as designed to secure freedom for local people from domination by this or that western power. The term that was used to describe such insurgents was usually something like 'guerrilla' or (if they looked as though they might succeed) 'freedom-fighter'. The complication in the Middle-East was that the Israelis (who had upon independence – and for reasons that are disputed to this day – taken possession of far more Palestinian land than the UN had intended) had neither any home country to which to return nor any desire to leave in any case. The first attempts to force Israel to concede a Palestinian state were entirely conventional, a model of how to conduct warfare on gentlemanly, Western-approved terms. In 1967 various state armies descended on Israel, hoping indeed to destroy it entirely or do it irreparable harm, but they were comprehensively repelled, with Israel seizing huge tracts of Jordan and Egypt in the process. The Palestinian Liberation Organisation then sought in a wholly traditional way to establish a guerrilla operation in these occupied territories from which to wage a 'war of liberation'. But their leader Yasser Arafat's ambitions to be the Michael Collins or Che Guevara of his people foundered on the ruthless implacability of the Israeli reaction: his fighters were being killed too easily, just as the soldiers of the national armies had been a short time before. It simply did not pay to try to fight Israel on equal terms: it was a kind of surrender with a simultaneous death sentence attached. So the Palestinians turned to isolated acts of political violence, by both official and renegade factions, on occasion very bloody it is true, but as not much more than a kind of consolation prize that had to be accepted because it was all that was available. It is in this sense that it is right to say that Arafat was a reluctant terrorist and in this sense it is also absolutely right to describe terrorism as 'the weapon of the weak'.[19]

The 1970s and 1980s were marked by high levels of violence in the region, in particular by the armed forces of the state of Israel but also, albeit to a much lesser extent, by Palestinian factions and as time went on (and particularly after the Iranian revolution in 1979) by more religiously-oriented movements such as Hezbollah and Islamic Jihad, working in southern Lebanon but also increasingly in the occupied territories themselves. During this period as well, some Palestinian factions took their fight to the streets and airports of Europe with occasional forays into extremely bloody violence

[19] The phrase is that of Walter Laqueur. See his *The Age of Terrorism* (Weidenfeld and Nicolson, London, 1987) where he makes this point about terrorism groups generally and not just the PLO.

indeed. But in any head count of casualties or any impartial assessment of levels of terror during this period, it is obvious that the lavishly equipped, well-organised and dominant military force in the region – the Israeli army – was responsible for by far the greatest numbers of killings and acts of politically motivated violence. If there were any doubt about this then all that needs to be recalled are the invasions of Lebanon that took place in 1978 and 1982, and in particular the two-month siege of Beirut that took place during the Summer of the latter year.[20] This was political terror by any ordinary definition of the term. Assisted by the internationalisation of the violence by some Palestinian factions which I mentioned a moment ago, a brilliantly successful campaign was then conducted by US and Israeli strategists and their academic and intellectual allies to castigate Palestinian violence as terrorist and therefore as uniquely evil. This had two powerful effects: first it disconnected Palestinian violence from its context and turned it into a more generalised problem, one that was faced by the Western World in general, rather than something that grew out of the injustice of the Israeli occupation. What helped here was that the generally very peaceful West was indeed suffering from occasional acts of subversive violence, from leftist ideological groups in Germany and Italy (the Red Brigades and the Baader-Meinhof gang respectively) and from irredentist nationalist groups in Corsica, Spain and Northern Ireland.[21] Even the

---

[20] R. Fisk, *Pity the Nation: Lebanon at War* (A. Deutsch, London, 1990) is a particularly harrowing account.

[21] The best general study of the terrorism of the period is A. Guelke, *The Age of Terrorism and the International Political System* (Tauris Academic Studies, I.B. Tauris Publishers, London, 1995).

United States had its own internal subversives, in the form of the Weathermen, afterwards the Weather Underground. All these groups became elided together under the general terrorist rubric, one within which in the 1970s the violent exponents of the Palestinian cause now also found themselves becoming helplessly enmeshed. 'Freedom-fighter' was long gone; 'guerrilla' and 'urban guerrilla' were fast becoming distant dreams. All the talk was of 'terrorists' and 'terrorism'.

Second, the same neat manoeuvre saw the Israeli defence forces identified with the counter-terrorist authorities in the West and therefore cast in the same sort of benign light – and this was regardless of the extreme, terror-inducing nature of their own violence, far in excess of what the US, British, Spanish etc. authorities were doing while coping with their own subversives. One book from this period for example, *Terrorism: How the West Can Win*, contained a contribution from Israel's ambassador to the United Nations Benjamin Netanyahu which described the 'war against terror' as 'part of a much larger struggle, one between the forces of civilization and the forces of barbarism'.[22] This volume – edited by Netanyahu who was also a leading 'terrorism expert' and was to become Israeli prime minister in due course – was published seven years before Samuel Huntingdon's famous article on the 'clash of civilisations'.[23] Taking advantage of the fact that Palestinian radicals struck outside Israel, institutes

---

[22] B. Netanyahu (ed.), *Terrorism: How the West Can Win* (Weidenfeld and Nicolson, London, 1986). See also B. Netanyahu, *Fighting Terrorism. How Democracies Can Defeat Domestic and International Terrorists* (Allison and Busby Ltd, London, 1996)

[23] S. Huntingdon, 'The Clash of Civilizations' 72 *Foreign Affairs* (1993) 22.

and think tanks were established to study the 'problem' of 'international terrorism': one such particularly influential organisation, the Jonathan Institute, held large conferences in Jerusalem in 1979 and in Washington in 1984, calling for the 'need for a better understanding of terrorism and for mobilizing the West against it.' The Institute was named after the Israeli commando who had died in the raid on Entebbe in 1976. After Iran began to support anti-Israeli forces in Lebanon, new studies began of 'state-sponsored terrorism' and if countries in the region fell out with the United States, they found themselves at risk of being classified as 'terrorist states' – a label that came and went as relations with Washington ebbed and flowed.[24]

The joint interest of the West and Israel in developing a common front against terrorism was consolidated in the 1980s. These were the Reagan years when pressure was being ratcheted up on the Soviet Union, or Evil Empire (as opposed to Axis of Evil) as it was then often quite unironically described. A succession of books and articles and terrorist commentaries made the link between the Soviet Union and the sponsorship of international terrorism in general and of the PLO in particular. This was the first global terrorist campaign of which, though now largely forgotten, so much was made at the time. Books with titles like *The Soviet Strategy of Terror*,[25] *The Grand*

---

[24] To the frustration of serious academics striving to impose order in the field: see G. Wardlaw, *Political Terrorism: Theory, Tactics and Counter-Measures* (Cambridge University Press, Cambridge, 2nd edn 1989), pp. 176–8.

[25] S.T. Francis, *The Soviet Strategy of Terror* (The Heritage Foundation, Washington DC, 1981).

Strategy of the Soviet Union,[26] *The Soviet Union and Terrorism,*[27] *The Soviet Connection: State Sponsorship of Terrorism*[28] and the evocatively titled *Hydra of Carnage*[29] flowed from the presses and the think-tanks. Especially influential was Clare Sterling's *The Terror Network: The Secret War of International Terrorism*, published by Weidenfeld and Nicolson in 1981.[30] The point being made by all this academic scholarship was that Soviet support for the Palestinian cause essentially made it a God-father of international terrorism the world over. So successful was this strategy of linkage between Palestinian actions and international terrorism that the attempted murder of the Israeli Ambassador to the UK in London in 1982 (by the Abu Nidhal faction) was capable of being made into a plausible *casus belli* of the invasion of Lebanon – Operation Peace in Galilee – which was launched two days later. But the invasion, and the siege of Beirut that followed, were not terrorism; they were counter-terrorism, and this was regardless of the terror that actually happened on the ground.

This framework for seeing the Israeli-Arab conflict, embedded so brilliantly in our public discourse in the 1970s, as

[26] E. Luttwak, *The Grand Strategy of the Soviet Union* (Weidenfeld and Nicolson, London, 1983).

[27] R. Goren, *The Soviet Union and Terrorism* (Allen and Unwin, London, 1984).

[28] J. Becker, *The Soviet Connection: State Sponsorship of Terrorism* (Institute for European and Defence and Strategic Studies, Occasional Paper No. 13, London, 1985).

[29] U. Ra'anan, R.L. Pfaltzgraff, R.H. Schultz, E. Halperin and I. Lukes, *Hydra of Carnage* (Lexington Books, Lexington, 1986).

[30] C. Sterling, *The Terror Network: the Secret War of International Terrorism* (Weidenfeld and Nicolson, London, 1981).

part of a worldwide contagion of irrational terror remains with us to this day. Of course the Soviet dimension has declined, but it has been replaced by a new pernicious supremo, radical Islam. Where once it was the Kremlin it is now Al Qaeda. The Politburo has been replaced by Osama Bin Laden, with brief stops for Abu Nidhal and President Gadaffi along the way. The transfer began to take place much earlier than is commonly understood, during the mid-1980s as Soviet power declined and political Islam asserted itself against western and Israeli interests, first in Iran (against the American-sponsored Shah) and later in Lebanon (against Israeli, US and French military forces buttressing the Christian regime in power in that country). In a book for the Institute for the Study of Conflict, entitled *The New Terrorism* and published as early as 1986, the terrorism expert William Gutteridge, sounded the following warning note about the future:

> The new wave of political violence in the Middle East and South Asia in the mid 1980s in which religious sectaranism is a potent factor has added other dangerous dimensions to the problem and at the same time focused attention sharply on the real danger to civilisation and international order which epidemic terrorism could pose.[31]

The point grew in substance with the increase in the 1990s both in violence within the occupied territories and in the outbreaks of political violence across the world from subversives now increasingly purporting to act in the name of Islam. This

---

[31] W. Gutteridge (ed.), *The New Terrorism* (Mansell Publishers, London, 1986).

was when Hamas got properly underway. Against this kind of background, it was not surprising that the attacks on 11 September came quickly to be seen as another part of the savage terrorist 'war' being waged by political Islam against the West in general and against that honorary part of the West, Israel, in particular. The government of Ariel Sharon repeated the triumph of an earlier generation of Israeli strategists in linking its private quarrel with the Palestinians to this global epidemic of terror. Speaking to the Knesset on 16 September 2001, the then Israeli Prime Minister put it in the following way:

> The subject of terror is unfortunately not new to us. The state of Israel has been fighting the Arab, Palestinian and Islamic fundamentalist's terror for over 120 years. Thousands of Jews have been murdered in terrorist attacks . . . The bereavement of the American people is known well to us.
>
> The war against terror has to be an international war. A war of the free world coalition against the forces of terror . . . It is a war between the humans and the blood thirsty.
>
> We know this as we have been in this battle for many years now.
>
> . . . We weren't surprised by the evilness of the Arab, Palestinian and radical Islamic terror. Arafat chose the strategy of terror and formed a coalition of terror. The terrorist attacks against Israeli citizens aren't any different than Bin Laden's terror attack against the American citizens- terror is terror.
>
> We must remember it was Arafat who gave the legitimacy to hijacking planes, and it was the Palestinian

terror groups that started sending suicide bombers. All the
radical movements got their legitimacy from Arafat . . .
    There is no such thing as terrorists who are 'good guys'
as there is no such thing as terrorists who are 'bad guys',
they are all bad.
    . . . I applaud President Bush for his decision to form a
coalition against terror. This coalition must fight all terror
organizations, including Arafat's . . .

As was the case in the 1980s, a large number of intellectuals,
politicians and non-governmental bodies promptly echoed this
theme of a new global war on Israel and the West, one which
embraced all elements of the Palestinian resistance as well as the
Al Qaeda 'terror network'.[32] In the resulting clash of civilisations, just as was the case in the 1970s and 1980s, there has never
been the space or time to consider carefully the context of any
of the sub-state political violence that is being scrutinised and
(inevitably) condemned. Proponents of this new global war
have had a high degree of success in persuading public opinion
that terrorism is a threat to the established order that is far more
serious than mere criminal acts and that it transcends whatever
local conditions might have given rise to it. In this way the violence of such insurgents is effectively isolated from its situation
and treated as immoral without further discussion. The 'terrorism' of the Middle-East is regarded as in some kind of way
the same as the 'terrorism' of the IRA, of ETA, and of all the
other subversive groups around the world. Security forces
everywhere are therefore engaged in the same kind of difficult

---

[32] See J. Burnett and D. Whyte, 'Embedded Expertise and the New
Terrorism' [2005] *Journal for Crime, Conflict and Media Culture* 1.

but essentially moral task – the saving of their people from 'terrorism' and from 'international terrorism'. Nothing further needs to be known – the pathology of terrorist violence needs to be identified and its supporters destroyed, wherever they are and regardless of any arguments that they might try to deploy to explain their position. What was true of the Palestinian Liberation Organisation in the 1970s and 1980s is also true of the militant groups to be found today in the occupied territories, in Afghanistan, in Iraq and elsewhere in the region. No attention, or no serious attention, needs to be paid to the political violence – by Israeli forces, by US forces, by other armies in the latest 'Coalition of the Willing' – which creates the conditions for this subversive violence and helps to ensure its perpetuation. There are literally no words left to describe state violence of this sort – all the truly bad words have been exclusively allocated to small, weak groups that cause a fraction of the fatalities of their more powerful opponents. But their mistake is to kill people like us.

Human rights and terrorism

The greatest violence the term 'terrorism' does to human rights is the way in which it frames the debate in the manner that I have just described. The primary effect of this is that it deprives the criminal justice model of the space with which to breath. This process is the epitome of good human rights practice. Crimes like murder, manslaughter and various other offences against the person put into practice the basic human rights to life and to bodily integrity. They also serve to make real the prohibitions on torture and inhuman and

123

degrading treatment that are to be found in most rights' charters. But charges are only brought against individuals against whom there is a reasonable suspicion of culpability, and punishment can only follow proof of guilt after a fair trial. Crucially from a human rights perspective, these crimes can be made to stick to state agents who break the law as well as other wrongdoers: on this model, torture or murder do not stop being torture or murder simply because somebody with a uniform happens to be doing the killing or torturing. In this way is a community's responsibility to protect its people reconciled with its duty to act fairly towards all those within its jurisdiction. At the national level, therefore, the criminal system is exactly the right one to deploy if it is desired to break the back of politically-motivated subversive violence within a democratic country. Its punishments are severe enough to matter while its focus on evidence, proof and fair procedures reduces the risk of miscarriages of justice without increasing the risk of dangerous disaffection on the part of those who might be tempted to follow the criminally-violent path. Of course if subversive violence is particularly serious, even a law-abiding state might feel the need to revisit its procedures to ensure that it has the balance right between individual fairness and public safety: rules of evidence and the procedures for calling witnesses or for guaranteeing jury safety cannot be rendered immutable to change. If particular criminal mischiefs call for international cooperation then this can be readily achieved via better cross-border policing and closer links between the executive arms of the various states with a common interest in tackling serious crime. If necessary UN agreements can be concluded on particular criminal concerns – the hijacking of planes; the illicit use of nuclear substances; transnational kidnapping. The point is to stay within the criminal framework throughout – it orients the state in the right direction, towards law enforcement, fair procedures and sensitive, evidence-driven policing. There is no need for the language of terrorism in any shape or form.

The terrorism model, though, blows a hole in this system. It disregards the criminal in favour of a language rooted in generalities which has little time for individual dignity or the rule of law. We have already alluded to the way in which UK law has drifted in this direction, with administrative powers rooted in executive judgments about involvement in terrorism (very broadly defined) being used against individuals and groups without the safeguards that would be regarded as normal if the criminal justice model were being followed. Human rights law in the United Kingdom has largely accommodated these security-oriented changes, and the effect of this has been to render them seemingly compliant with rather than inherently hostile to human rights principles. This has been achieved by a combination of, on the one hand, a code of human rights law that concedes within itself the need for occasional state action to safeguard national security and, on the other, an executive branch that has been sensitive to the need to give up some of the power it wants in order to secure a satisfactory human rights outcome.[33] So in Britain we have long periods of pre-charge detention on suspicion, albeit overseen by a judicial officer on the basis of rather general criteria

---

[33] For further details, see C.A. Gearty, '11 September 2001, Counter-terrorism and the Human Rights Act' 32 *Journal of Legal Studies* (2005) 18. Cf. K.D. Ewing, 'The Futility of the Human Rights Act' [2004] *Public Law* 829.

sympathetic to state necessity.[34] There is an executive power to ban political associations but an independent tribunal (albeit without the security of a court) to which affected organisations can appeal.[35] The anti-terrorism control orders provided for in the terrorism law enacted in 2005 by way of a response to the Belmarsh decision accept the need for some judicial safeguards, albeit these do appear very weak when looked at from a criminal perspective. And so on. Some believe that this packaging of terrorism law in a kind of ersatz due process is merely brilliant salesmanship, a clever way of attacking human rights while seemingly to comply with them, of salving the conscience of New Labour authoritarians. I have said as much myself recently, likening such safeguards to 'confetti at a funeral'.[36] It is certainly right that we would be better off with an improved code of criminal law outlining specific offences and providing mainstream procedural safeguards against abuse. At another level, however, this entanglement of terrorism law in the criminal process, and in particular the use of judges and lawyers from the historically independent legal professions to make it work, may over time transform such alien codes into something which much more closely resembles ordinary criminal law than it does at present. Given that it is unlikely that the terrorism laws are going to disappear anytime soon, this is certainly a goal worth working towards.

And where would you prefer to be a suspected terrorist, London or Washington? Before we critics of the United

---

[34] Terrorism Act 2000, part V.   [35] Terrorism Act 2000, part II.

[36] C.A. Gearty, 'Human Rights in an Age of Counter-Terrorism: Injurious, Irrelevant or Indispensable?' 58 *Current Legal Problems* (2005) 25, at p. 31.

Kingdom's determination to make terrorism law human rights compatible become too shrill in our attacks, we should look to the United States to see what happens when no such efforts are made. In that jurisdiction of course there are no human rights as such to control the security instincts of the federal authorities, but there is supposed to be the Constitution and guaranteeing its omnipotence, and thereby the supremacy of the rule of law, is supposed to be the main task of the US Supreme Court. Aspects of the Bush administration's response to the attacks of 11 September 2001 have mimicked the British in that efforts have been made to secure legislative changes which have empowered the authorities to act in certain new – and undeniably draconian – ways. This is playing the game essentially by the old rules: you push something through Congress before you do what it will empower you to do, and you hope that the powers will not be struck down by the courts. The highly controversial Patriot Act is a good example. But it is now clear that this was only a small part of the administration's response, and that in fact the major commitment was to executive action without the authority of any law whatsoever. There are echoes here of the ominous Operation Kratos under which British police secretly agreed new terms of engagement to deal with potential suicide bombers and almost immediately ended up killing an innocent man. Since shortly after the 11 September attacks the National Security Agency in the United States has been empowered by presidential order to monitor international telephone calls and e-mails of US citizens and residents without the warrant from the secret foreign intelligence court that is requird by law. It is estimated that hundreds, perhaps thousands, of people have been under such surveillance. According to the President this is a 'limited program' aimed at those suspected of having links with terrorism and that it is 'vital and necessary' to protect the country.[37] These may be good arguments as to why there should be such a law, but these are not reasons in themselves for bypassing the law-making process altogether. The language of terrorism provides the justification for these egregious breaches of the right to privacy and (as far as Operation Kratos is concerned) the right to life: they could not have arisen if we had stuck to the criminal model.

Lacking the enforcement arm of a state, international law has been even easier to ignore than domestic law. In November 2005, the Pentagon conceded that the United States had detained more than 80,000 people in facilities from Afghanistan to Cuba since the attacks on 11 September.[38] A large proportion of the 500 or so detainees being held at Guantanamo are believed to be on hunger strike and are being forcibly fed by the authorities.[39] Naturally enough there are lawyers who can be found who will argue that the US policy of detentions is in accord with international law, just as there are some who say that the president can do what he wants within the jurisdiction as well. Fortunately they are few and far between. Unfortunately they occupy positions of immense power.[40] And their opinions dovetail nicely with the prejudices of their bosses. For it has to be acknowledged that

---

[37] *Washington Post* 2 January 2006, p. A2.
[38] *Guardian* 18 November 2005.   [39] *Guardian* 19 November 2005.
[40] The definitive account is M. Danner, *Torture and Truth. America, Abu Ghraib and the War on Terror* (Granta Books, London, 2005). There is a good summary by A. Lewis in *The Nation*, 26 December 2005, pp. 13–15.

scepticism about the rule of law goes right to the very heart of this American administration. As President Bush said in his State of the Union Address in 2004, 'It is not enough to serve our enemies with legal papers.' Even more brutally to the point, this is how Secretary Rumsfeld put it in the 2005 *National Defence Strategy of the United States*: 'Our strength as a nation state will continue to be challenged by those who employ a strategy of the weak using international fora, judicial processes, and terrorism.'[41] If you took this quote, located it in the twentieth rather than early twenty-first Century and asked an informed audience who had said it, I wonder which characters would spring first to mind? American names would not be likely to be first on the list.

And then of course there is the torture. It is an important part of the US sense of itself that the country is not a place where torture has ever been officially or even unofficially contemplated. This is to put it mildly – and contra the idealists like Senator John McCain – ahistorical. Torture has directly and through its proxies been integral to US foreign policy since the Vietnam War. Mechanisms of no-touch torture based on sensory deprivation and self-inflicted pain were developed as part of the Phoenix program during that conflict and were then exported to Latin America and Asia under the guise of police training programs.[42] The School of Americas based in Panama from 1946 until 1984 became so notorious that it was thought

[41] See K.J. Greenberg, 'Secrets and Lies' *The Nation* 26 December 2005, p. 40.

[42] See Alfred McCoy, *A Question of Torture* (forthcoming), discussed at length by N. Klein, ' "Never Before!" Our Amnesiac Torture Debate' *The Nation* 26 December 2005, pp. 11–12.

wiser to relocate the establishment to Fort Benning, Georgia. What was new after 11 September was the openness with which the previously covert policy was now being promulgated. Memos and legal opinions began to flow from the administration which argued that the President, in his constitutional role as commander-in-chief, had the power to order torture whatever the domestic law might say. It was also asserted that the Geneva Conventions did not apply to the unlawful combatants held by the US authorities, and that the Convention against Torture did not apply to actions against non-Americans outside the United States. It was also suggested that torture was not after all quite what everybody else believed: conduct could be described as such only where it produced pain equivalent to that from 'serious physical injury, such as organ failure, impairment of bodily function, or even death'. Anything else – no matter how awful – simply wasn't torture.[43]

The details of the various moves that the Bush White House has made away from democratic accountability, the rule of law and human dignity, all in the name of the 'Global War on Terror' that it says it has to fight, need not detain us here. The challenge to human rights is manifest. We have already seen how the discourse of terrorism challenges universality and by positing a version of the world rooted in good and evil makes possible the kinds of subversions of our subject that I have been discussing. Our interest at this juncture lies in the reaction that these attacks on our human rights – liberty, bodily integrity, life and so on – have provoked from human rights defenders. The majority of progressives and public intellectuals have been fierce

---

[43] See generally Danner, n. 40 above.

in their denunciations. But this has not been a unanimous response by any means. A substantial number of lawyers, media commentators and academics, particularly in the United States, have supported, either in whole or in part, the actions of the administration. Many of these have been supposed 'human rights experts', professors and lawyers allegedly well-versed in the requirements of their subject. This is not to say that they all give the Bush White House carte blanche; enough differences are maintained for critical distance to continue to appear to be preserved. And they disagree among themselves as well. Some of them do not go as far as others in what they would permit: at their conferences and in each other's edited books they argue among themselves about the morality of this or that kind of sensory deprivation and sometimes they even come down against indefinite detention without charge.[44] The details matter less than the fact of the discussions: internment, torture, coercive interrogation, covert surveillance and other manifestations of lawless state power are not any longer simple wrongs to be avoided and severely punished when they occur; rather they have become a set of proposed solutions to supposed ethical

---

[44] Among the books recently published on the subject are: S. Levinson (ed.), *Torture. A Collection* (Oxford University Press, Oxford, 2004); R.A. Wilson, *Human Rights in the 'War on Terror'* (Cambridge University Press, Cambridge, 2005); K. Roth and M. Worden (eds.), *Torture. Does It Make Us Safer? Is it Ever Ok?* (The New Press, Human Rights Watch, New York, 2005); A.M. Dershowitz, *Why Terrorism Works: Understanding the Threat, Responding to the Challenge* (Yale University Press, New Haven, 2002). For a comprehensive guide to those who have supported torture or some forms of what has in the past been thought to be ill-treatment, see 'The Torture Tree' published in *The Nation* 26 December 2005, pp. 28–29.

dilemmas that need now to be considered and debated, as you might consider and debate any other kind of policy proposal. The unspeakable is no longer unspoken. Even the greatest of our human rights taboos – the prohibition on torture and inhuman and degrading treatment – has become just another point of view – and to some people an eccentrically absolutist one at that.

It is not hard to see how President Bush, Vice-President Cheney and Secretary Rumsfeld have taken such a position. But how have a substantial number of liberal progressives and human rights intellectuals coped with taking such a line? This is where the war on terror plays its part – it supplies the 'ethical dilemma' from which all else flows. Those who take the line I have just outlined tend also to accept the idea of a global campaign of terrorism that threatens us all. This leads them to see human rights not as a subject concerned with the powerless individual wherever he or she might be in the world but rather as an idea which finds its clearest expression in the West, indeed as something highly particular to the West, one of the reasons why it considers its culture to be superior to that of others. In this way the 'human' is taken out of 'human rights', the particular is superseded by the general, and the subject becomes one that is more about values than it is about people. On this analysis respect for human rights becomes this abstract thing that we in the West have which we must defend against those who would by destroying our culture also wreck this precious but vulnerable commitment. Michael Ignatieff's recent book *The Lesser Evil* is perhaps the best example of the genre.[45] To

---

[45] *The Lesser Evil. Political Ethics in an Age of Terror* (Edinburgh University Press, Edinburgh, 2004).

Ignatieff, we are faced with 'evil' people and 'either we fight evil with evil or we succumb'. 'Terrorist movements like Al Qaeda or Hamas are death cults' and it 'is redemption they are after, and they seek death sure that they have attained it'. The 'we' here is unavoidable because pervasive: intellectuals like Michael Ignatieff writing about the dangers of terrorism are speaking for the decent 'West' against a horrible other; it is a conversation with friends about what to do about the neighbour from hell. And it needs to be said that in these accounts of good and evil Israel always figures in the Western family. Just as in the 1970s global war on terror against the 'Evil Empire', Israel is our friend, the bastion of our values in a hostile zone, a beacon of good in a region of evil.

Once these assumptions about terrorism and good and evil are accepted, it becomes clear that the western/Israeli democracies are indeed entitled to do some wrong in their struggle for survival. The human rights justification goes along the following lines. Unlike the terrorists, the defenders of democracy know that what they are doing (say they have to do) is wrong (or at least a bit wrong) even when they are doing it, and they have a set of democratic values to hand to stop things getting out of control. Those values commit them to respecting the moral status of human beings and to guaranteeing 'to respect the rights of those who have shown no respect for rights at all, to show mercy to those who are merciless, [and] to treat as human those who have behaved inhumanly'.[46] But, precisely because we democratic people are special in this way, value everybody so highly and

[46] *Ibid.* p. 34.

133

so on, 'necessity may require us to take actions in defence of democracy which will stray from democracy's own foundational commitments to dignity'.[47] So if we change our rules to allow us to respond in an evil way, or our operatives stray over the boundary into evil behaviour without our explicit authorisation, it is really not so bad (fine even?) because all that is happening is that evil is being met with (lesser/theoretically accountable) evil. Indeed it is hard to be at all angry with (much less punish) 'the carnivores who disgrace the society they are charged to protect'[48] when what they are doing is protecting us not merely from our political opponents, nor even only from our enemies, but rather from evil itself. Our evil is better (because less bad) than theirs. If Abu Ghraib was wrong, then that wrongness consisted not in stepping across the line into evil behaviour but rather allowing a 'necessary evil' (as framed by the intellectuals) to stray into 'unnecessary evil' (as practised by the military on the ground).

Exactly this kind of human rights language has also played a part in the invasion of Iraq. A kind of militant humanitarianism had grown up during the late 1990s which had argued for a more robust strategy of intervention to secure human rights goals in faraway lands. This had led many liberals to support the US attacks on Afghanistan which followed the 11 September attacks.[49] While Stephen Holmes is right when he says that the 'heady support' of 'certain sparkling intellects . . . played little or no role in the

---

[47] *Ibid.* p. 8.   [48] *Ibid.* p. 144.
[49] D. Chandler, *From Kosovo to Kabul and Beyond. Human Rights and International Intervention* (Pluto Press, London, New edn 2006).

decision to invade Iraq' he is also correct to note that 'it did diminish and isolate voices of dissent'.[50] Had the Iraqi occupation turned out as Washington strategists intended, there can be little doubt that the focus would now be on Syria's abysmal human rights record and its unlawful interference with Lebanon's affairs. The threat of military action would probably by now have been ratcheted up against Iran in light particularly of its apparent effort to secure nuclear weapons – a hardly surprising policy choice it must be said given what has been happening in recent years in its two neighbouring countries, Iraq and Afghanistan. (How would the US react if Mexico and Canada were invaded and occupied by Iranian forces in possession of weapons of mass destruction of which it had none?) But we can be equally sure in this hypothetical future following a successful pacifying of Iraq that about Israel there would not have been a single murmur from the administration or its intellectual supporters : its development of nuclear weapons capacity would have remained unpunished, its illegal occupation of Palestinian land would have gone largely unnoticed, its invasion of neighbouring countries still a thing of the past to be glossed over or forgotten. The human rights militants who would have been in the front row demanding action against Syria and Iran would have justified their silence on Israel by asserting that it is a country that subscribes to human rights values and that it is engaged in necessary evil against a global terrorist enemy, and that therefore its actions are morally better even when objectively they look a whole lot worse.

[50] 'The War of the Liberals' *The Nation* 14 November 2005, p. 29.

Conclusion: human rights fights back

In order to ensure its survival, the human rights idea needs to stand firmly against this kind of distortion of its essence, this move to turn it into a basis for selective aggression abroad and an alibi for brutality at home. The moment the human rights discourse moves into the realm of good and evil is the moment when it has fatally compromised its integrity. For once these grand terms are deployed in the discussion, all bets are off as far as equality of esteem is concerned. If we are good and they are bad, then of course equality of esteem as between all of us is ludicrous. Why esteem the evildoer in the same way as he or she who does good? These are not now any longer human beings *simpliciter* but different kinds of humans: one good, one bad. The latter, being evil, are not only different, but worse, worse even than animals who are, after all, incapable of evil. The wonder is not that we good guys abuse their human rights but that we continue to use such language in relation to them at all, recognise that they have any residual human rights worth noticing. And who is this 'they' that fill the category of lesser (because evil) humans? In theory of course the Bush administration and the liberal advocates of necessary evil agree that it is just the members of the terrorist brigades, the few truly rotten apples intent on destroying all that we civilised, good people stand for. In the absence of a sensible code of law (boring things like the presumption of innocence, independent trials and the like – mere pedantry in the face of evil!), we have no way of telling which non-Westerners are entirely evil and which merely evil by (involuntary?) association. The easiest thing to do is to suspect the whole targeted community of being evil, and after that – because we have dispensed with procedural mechanisms for proof – it is inevitable that that suspicion, simply through repetition, should mature into a firm conviction – but it remains one without any serious evidential base whatsoever, a conviction of the moral warrior not a court of law. It affects whole civilisations, tarring them with the stigma of an evil theoretically designed only for the baddest of the very bad within.

Again we are back with the single greatest disastrous legacy of the war on terror from a human rights point of view, the supersession of the criminal model based on justice and due process by a security model that is based on fear and suspicion. One of the great achievements of international law has been to remove the language of good and evil from the relationship between states. The 'just war' theory having the rather fatal flaw that 'justice' is in the eye of the beholder, it was thought far better to tie states down to specific rules and treaties into which morality (rival versions of good and evil) did not stray.[51] International humanitarian and human rights law represented the apogee of this civilizing trend in global affairs, with rules of decent conduct that took their colour from the fact of our shared humanity rather than the superiority of our particular cause being agreed and promulgated. Now, thanks primarily to the crude actions of this American administration but also to the willingness of important liberals to embrace the language, we are back in a pre-rule phase where, in effect, despite the liberals' best hopes, anything goes. What is good for one side is good for the other as well, so we

---

[51] G. Oberleitner, 'A Just War Against Terror' 16 *Peace Review* (2004) 263.

have seen a bleak escalation in the inhumanity shown towards Western captives, towards aid workers and others – journalists, support staff – working in the theatre of war. Various axes of evil bestride the world, with the exact centres of evil depending entirely on where you are standing.

The war on terror has already done serious damage to the integrity of human rights, turning our subject into a kind of moral mask behind which lurk cruelty and oppression. But the signs are that the mood is turning and that resistance to this narrative is gathering momentum. The furore over extraordinary rendition that has taken up so much attention recently is in some ways good news, especially allied to the strong anti-torture assertions made by the Secretary of State Dr Rice during a visit to Europe in December 2005. It seems that under the pressure of Abu Ghraib and conceding a little in the face of international opinion, the administration has returned to the traditional US approach to torture, that of plausible deniability. In an imperfect world this realisation that it is embarrassing that you admit to torture must count as a moral advance. Even better would be a move, possibly lead by the European Union[52] or the Council of Europe, for far better enforcement of the Convention against Torture, and for the punishment of those states – allegedly some of them European – that have facilitated the US desire to ill treat captives in a deniable way.[53] Elements within the legislative, the judicial and even the executive branches of both the United States and the United

[52] 'EU threat to countries with secret CIA prisons' *Guardian* 29 November 2005.

[53] See M. Bright, 'Rendition: the Cover-Up' *New Statesman* 23 January 2006, pp. 12–13.

Kingdom have become more voluble of late, subjecting assertions of terrorist threats and claims about danger to national
security to more scrutiny than has been the case in the past.[54]
Perhaps this is a consequence of the exposure of the faultiness
of much of the intelligence with which the general public in
both countries were persuaded to back the invasion and occupation of Iraq. These are advances that can be built on. But the
subject of human rights will not be truly safe until the language
of terrorism, and with it all dangerous talk of good and evil, is
removed entirely from political rhetoric and from national and
international law, to be replaced with (as far as the first is concerned) a more nuanced approach to international relations
and (in relation to the second) a code of law that emphasises
the primacy of the criminal model over that of emergency or
national security driven approaches. And for either of these
outcomes to be regarded even as possibilities, a just solution
must first be found to the political problems in Palestine and
Israel.

[54] Thus both the UK Parliament and the US Senate have recently taken
liberal initiatives, on detention and torture respectively. Judicial
authorities in both jurisdictions have handed down decisions that have
overturned executive policy in sensitive anti-terrorism areas, most
recently in Britain in relation to the use that can be made (or rather not
made) of torture evidence: *A v Secretary of State for the Home
Department (No. 2)* [2005] UKHL 71. Even the UK executive has been
slowly relenting on its steadfast refusal to allow intercept evidence to be
used in court: see 'Free foreign suspects on control orders, says terror
watchdog' *Guardian* 3 February 2006.

5

Can human rights survive?

In this book my goal has been to rethink the subject of human rights so as to enable it to survive the challenges to its integrity, indeed to its very existence, that have emerged off the back of its recent, great success. Coping with the three crises that I discuss in chapters 2 to 4 has been central to this project. Successfully steering our way past these encounters with authority, with legalism and with national security has meant than now, as this book nears its end, we are ready to resume our human rights journey, but with greater confidence than in the past about where we are going and with a better sense also of the pitfalls that need to be avoided in future. The key point has been to recognise what at its core our subject is about, what the essence is from which all else flows. We have seen that at its heart, the idea of human rights is two-dimensional. There is the absolute side – the moral wrongness of cruelty and humili-ation, and there is also the – perhaps less clear but nevertheless essential – dedication to human flourishing. The two are linked in that each flows from a commitment to human dignity, which is in turn manifested in acts of compassion towards the other. In its prohibitory form, this demands that we do not degrade our fellow humans by depersonalising them. The positive side. stressing growth and personal success, sees human rights as radically pluralist in the hospitality towards others – rather than mere tolerance of them – that its underlying ethic demands. Viewed as a whole, therefore, human rights is an idea that both protects us as persons and enables us to grow at the same time.

Marx thought that a world of individuals isolated from each other, deprived of their true humanity by the brute force of market-based circumstances, was what human rights was all about. This may have been the case in the past, a point I have developed in chapter 3. But today, nothing could be further from the truth. Marx's vision may be a good description of our current, globalised world but if this is indeed the case, then human rights are rightly cast as subversive rather than supportive of such a brutal status quo. As chapter 2 showed, human rights is concerned with valuing each of us for what we are, and what we are is not just an autonomous, organic entity separate from everything around us but rather a self that is located – located in a family, a community, a nation, an ethnic group – and it is precisely through our circle of various belongings that we can flourish as persons, lead successful lives as full human beings, and fulfil the promise of human rights. Our subject is not about the individual versus the state and everybody else, nor is it about rights without responsibilities; rather it is about the freedom that flows from the solidarity of reciprocated esteem, from the enrichment that is made possible by multiple belongings, each facilitating our success as persons but none superior to the different routes that are chosen by others whose particular life circumstances make these other pathways to success more natural for them to navigate. As a joint submission to a UK government review put it at the end of 2005, 'the human rights vision of equality extends significantly beyond discrimination . . . to encompass fairness of treatment, dignity, respect and access to the fundamental rights which enable participation in a democratic society.'[1]

Our subject can meet the challenges of legalism and national security head on by avoiding being manoeuvred into the cul-de-sac of legal legitimisation ('it is not a breach of article X so it must be all right!') or national chauvinism ('the country is at stake so anything goes!') and stressing instead these basic points about human solidarity, the need to avoid cruelty, the commitment to diversity and plurality, and the promotion of well-being. And it can answer the challenge to its foundational authority, to its truth in a world of uncertainty, by saying – as we said at the end of chapter 2 – that doubt can be appreciated, celebrated even, without being given a veto over all moral progress, and that in any event to doubt is not to know: scepticism is better than fact-based hostility, the agnostic a more attractive foe (because closer to us than he or she can know) than the well-briefed atheist. To resist all three challenges successfully, it is important that the idea of human rights should never lose sight of its essential particularity: it is about *individual* humans not great political systems. As we saw in chapter 4, it is when we seek to defend human rights not as a particular form of individual justice but as some abstract thing which our culture has and others don't that we end up with the horrors of Abu Ghraib and Guantanamo Bay: cruelty to protect us from cruelty; oppression to ensure the success of tolerance; killing to secure the freedom of our victims.

[1] F. Klug, H. Wildbore, K. Ghose and A. Edmundson, *Evidence to the Equalities Review from the British Institute of Human Rights and the Centre for the Study of Human Rights, LSE.*

Throughout this book, the idea of human rights has been conceived as a kind of mask that our society can choose to put on. In chapter 2, the mask is essential and wholly benign; we wear it to advertise our commitment to human rights values and to declare the moral importance of our human rights obligations. This mask is vital because, while we like the idea and respect enormously what it stands for, some of us are not so sure any more that human rights can any longer be shown to be 'objectively' true or indeed that they can be rooted in any kind of fact. This mask of moral obligation protects us from our doubting selves: for those not ready to accept any blame of universalism it is a deception that is chosen rather than one that needs to be shaken off. The mask in chapter 3 is, in contrast, partly benign: it is the law's claim to speak with authority on what human rights actually are, and then to make its version of the idea real by its power of direction to the organs of the state. But as we saw in that chapter, the law can sometimes get it wrong, and in particular that its version of what human rights entails has the potential to be subversive of true human rights, in particular to that part of the subject concerned with human flourishing. So the mask of legality ought to be capable of being torn aside where the public want to be certain that they can achieve a particular kind of human flourishing, one the human rights dimension to which the lawyers and judges cannot be trusted to spot and protect. In contrast to each of our first two masks, the disguise worn by human rights in chapter 4 is wholly malign: it puts a human rights gloss on cruelty, oppression and domination, allowing those who promote and practise such degrading acts to present themselves as, despite everything, committed to the human rights ideal. Our subject has no need for this mask – in chapter 4 we have argued it should be ripped aside and discarded before it destroys the subject for good.

Thinking about the way in which the language of human rights is being distorted leads us to the agenda for action that I promised earlier, a way of rebuilding the language of human rights before it is too late. With the structures right, the idea of human rights can make progress, showing it is not rendered immobile by doubt and that it is hostage neither to the deadening hand of the law nor to the imperatives of a colonially-minded national interest. To succeed in this way, it must not be an easy subject: the human rights tent should not be so broad that everybody can be squeezed into it, and some interest groups and advocates will be surprised, angry indeed, to be left outside. Those who argue passionately that there is a human right to incite others to hatred, whether of a religious or a racist or (I would say) of any other variety, are surely not entitled to be first in the queue for our solicitude and support. For is there not something wrong with a movement, one supposedly rooted in esteem and human dignity, that nevertheless finds its most pressing task to be the protection of hate-mongers in the public arena? This may have been worth doing in generations past when powerful and repressive religions needed more than ridicule to bring them down. But they are long gone now, whereas hate, inspired by fear and hurled along by anger, is in the driving-seat. Human rights should be slowing hate down not helping it on its way. In recent discussions about the enactment of an incitement to religious hatred law in the United Kingdom, great anxiety has been expressed about the stifling effect on free speech of such a provision. But the law proposed to and ultimately accepted in a modified form by Parliament contained its own safeguard in that prosecutions could not be launched other than by the relevant public authority. Even if the law had been passed in its original form there would have been no outburst of legal vigilantism. Nor would there have been any open season on comedians, writers and the like: the words 'incitement' and 'hatred' do far more controlling work than critics have allowed, transforming the provision not only in its enacted but also in its original form into one that is protective of the human rights ideal. True, some hate speech will be controlled, but despite what many liberals and lawyers often assert, free speech is not what human rights is entirely about: it is part of the subject, an important part certainly, but not one so central that hatemongering must be protected whatever the consequences.

One area where freedom of speech does need to be looked at afresh, and where human rights advocates could more usefully direct their energies, lies in managing the impact of new technology, in particular the internet. There are many issues here: the control of the system by the United States of America; the impact on privacy as well as on freedom of information of this new system of communication; the attempts by some governments, most notably the Chinese, to block access to sensitive internet sites within its jurisdiction; above all, perhaps, the digital divide that is fast growing between poor and rich countries. The World Summit on the Information Society held in Tunis in November 2005 recognised the importance of civil society to deliberations on these various challenges, according equal status to civil society as to governments. It is a pity that a stronger human rights perspective was not brought to the occasion, by for example pointing out that politically repressed Tunisia was hardly the right place to hold a celebration of free speech ('the diplomatic equivalent of booking Brixton town hall for the National Front's annual get-together' was how the *Guardian* described it.[2]) These kinds of issues are difficult but they are what set the ethical framework for the future. Books like that edited by Matthias Klang and Andrew Murray on *Human Rights in the Digital Age*[3] should be required reading for all those interested in the future good health of our subject. It is these future battlegrounds that human rights supporters should be identifying and occupying, not wasting valuable time and energy re-fighting old wars.

Progressive human rights thinking should also not be afraid to look honestly at what is meant by human life. Past quarrels litter this field as well, making clear thinking particularly difficult. It seems obvious that the flourishing of each of us, but of the girls and women among us in particular, can be greatly stunted by a parenthood that is initially unplanned and which is then largely unsupported by state and civil society alike. Many a woman's life is crushed by the responsibility of unsought motherhood, a duty discharged as best it can be even by those reluctant to take it on, but at a huge cost to such women's personal and future well-being. A true human rights culture would embrace the capacity of man and woman alike to enjoy their sexuality as a wonderful and (as compared with other animals) unexpected part of what it means to be human. But it would teach also the importance of self-respect and the wrongness of using any other person instrumentally for the

---

[2] *Technology Guardian* 24 November 2005, p. 6
[3] M. Klang and A. Murray (eds.), *Human Rights in the Digital Age* (London, Glasshouse Press, Cavendish Publishing, 2005).

servicing of transient sexual needs. Birth control and where necessary the termination of a very recently created foetus might well be essential parts of this human rights agenda. But at a certain stage in a pregnancy, the dignity of the unborn would need also to be recognised, not as a route to the upholding of this or that religious dictate or as a way of smuggling in an absolute bar on abortion, or trying further to oppress women, but rather as a reflection of the fact, shown by today's science, that we can feel pain and suffer grievously long before we leave our mother's womb. Of course unwanted babies are a terrible disaster, for the babies themselves as well as for the mothers who unwillingly have them: but there must be better ways of protecting such mothers from the stunting of their lives than by reliance on an operation that is too often routine when it should be a desperate last step.

It is also time for the human rights movement to take a view on the right to die, and on euthanasia generally. There does seem to be an unanswerable case for 'living wills', for decisions made by fully functioning adults at the prime of their lives as to how they want to die, and in particular as to how much effort at a future date should be devoted to keeping them alive. Such instruments should also be capable of requesting 'assisted suicides' without exposing those who carry out such wishes to criminal sanction. In the ancient law on wills, we have a template for ensuring that the use of such documentation does not become the subject of abuse. But living wills aside, can we argue seriously for a right to terminate a life when we know that advances in palliative care now make it possible for all in our culture to depart this life in a pain-free way, and when we can see that whatever hedges we place around the subject by allowing our elderly to choose to die we will be putting enormous moral pressure on those who choose not to? The old, the debilitated, the tired and aged – a natural constituency, we might think, for human rights support – might find instead that all the talk is not of their protection and support but of their having the right to die, a right that in the mind of the already vulnerable could quickly disintegrate into an obligation to depart. A 'living will' signed in such circumstances might resemble more a coercively induced loss of the will to live than a mature judgment about the right way to die.

There are also real human rights dilemmas about genetic technology. Clearly there is much good work being done here, with many lives being made incalculably richer by having been able to avail of advances in scientific practice that would have been unthinkable only a few years ago. But the old argument about a 'slippery slope' and the usually tired question 'how far can you go?' have real saliency here. Clear human rights thinking can help us to draw the line. Certainly 'designer babies', even – *in extremis* but not scientifically out of the question – cloned children and the like can add to the flourishing of those humans whose wants give rise to them. But let us ask the question honestly: what is the price paid by 'equality of esteem' for the new liberal eugenics argued for by so many? Once we depart from the premise of human life as a wonderful though unpredictable gift and replace the life we are given with the one we choose to have, have we not made an enormous breach in the core assumption that lies behind human rights, that we are all to be celebrated for what we are, not for the attributes that we bring with us to our lives? This is not necessarily a religious insight: even if our belief in human rights is rooted in awe at the mere fact of our existence, is this sense of wonder not ruptured by so direct a manipulation of what we are? I cannot see how gene technology if uncontrolled can avoid transforming our vision of ourselves as a gift of nature and turning us instead into things made by us, the product of our needs not the consequence of our shared humanity.

This is a challenging agenda but if it is to survive, human rights needs to develop a cutting edge, the confidence to shrink its tent, to leave people outside, to say this is the 'human rights programme' and it may not be to the liking of all. It is only when a set of political ideas has made serious enemies that it can be said to be making moral progress. On the international front, the link with liberal progressiveness is perhaps easier to maintain. Manifestly the UN human rights institutions need reform – the replacement body for the old, largely disgraced Commission for Human Rights should now get back to preventing human rights abuses and stop offering asylum to human rights abusers. Proponents of human rights protection across the world are often accused of being overly critical of the US and other Western powers, ignoring the plight of victims of human rights abuses in less open societies. This criticism needs to be taken on board, and it can be answered to a degree by the mustering of very strong human rights support for change at the UN – a strong, independent and authoritative new human rights presence would be the single most effective way of putting pressure on human-rights-abusing regimes across the world. Enthusiasts for human rights tend to be activist in inclination, impatient of diplomacy and of the compromises required for the development of effective, long-term political strategies. Often an advantage, this 'action first' attitude of the human rights (for want of a better word) 'community' is not helpful when it comes to structural reform. If it is serious about making real, substantial and enduring progress, the human rights movement needs to be less morally superior, more prepared to climb down from its ethical perch and muck in with the kind of people (diplomats, politicians) whom it has historically (often for good reason it must be said) disdained. Human rights organisations should also strive themselves to be 'whiter than white' setting codes of best practice for their own internal affairs, committing themselves to high levels of budgetary transparency and generally behaving in a way that is even better than what they demand of others.

Thus invigorated and with a confident understanding of their place in the world, proponents of the human rights idea would be well-placed to make a contribution to the two greatest ethical challenges facing the world today, poverty and environmental destruction. The single greatest mockery of our subject is the extent to which the gulf in resources between rich and poor has continued to deepen even while we in the developed world have been celebrating more and more our commitment to global human rights. According to the UN more than 850 million people, of whom 300 million are children, go hungry every day. Six million children die of malnourishment every year. In Africa alone, more than 40 per cent of the people do not have the ability to secure sufficient food on a daily basis.[4] This is where the human rights mask is at its most dangerous, as a piece of moral clothing which permits those of us

---

[4] See *International Cooperation at a Crossroads: Aid, Trade and Security in an Unequal World* (UNDP Human Development Report, Oxford University Press, 2005), ch. 1.

who are well-off in the affluent parts of the world to continue contentedly to live in our cocoon of privilege, one that is however – if we are being honest with ourselves – positively dependant on injustice elsewhere, on a refusal to share and on a twisting of trade rules to suit ourselves. A true commitment to human rights needs to pierce this veil of deluded complacency, to show that it is not enough to believe, to care in the abstract, but that it is also important to act. Only then can we meet the criticisms of those who deride human rights as an empty ideology, one designed to preserve rather than to uproot injustice and inequality. Even within the developed world itself, the gulf between rich and poor remains disgraceful from a human rights perspective. According to a recent and authoritative study by Professor John Hills of LSE, Britain has become a dramatically more unequal society in the last quarter century, with two-fifths of the total growth in personal disposable incomes since 1979 having gone to the richest tenth of the population.[5] Speaking at the launch of his book, Hills warned that the 'tax and spending dilemmas facing policymakers are likely to become more acute over coming decades. They face an uncomfortable trade-off between accepting rising costs and taxes in the long-term, reductions in generosity that increase poverty, or changes in structure that increase reliance on means testing and reduce the value of services for those with middle incomes.' It is obvious where proponents of human rights should be positioned in this debate: pointing out that the flourishing of the few cannot be bought at the price of the many, and that poverty is a social contrivance which not

[5] John Hills, *Inequality and the State* (Oxford University Press, Oxford, 2004).

only degrades its victims but also makes their enjoyment of their basic rights well-nigh impossible.

Most important of all, the human rights movement needs to confront the challenge of the environment. The UN's Intergovernmental Panel on Climate Change (IPCC) has produced three assessment reports, in 1990, 1995 and 2001, with a fourth due in 2007. The third of these reports contained many serious warnings about the need for urgent action on climate change but its pessimism on the subject was dwarfed by the findings of the interim assessment team which were presented at a meeting in Exeter in February 2005. Two developments in particular shocked those who were present.[6] First, there is now a real possibility that the vast West Antarctic Ice Sheet is beginning to break up. If it does go, global sea levels would rise by 16 feet, destroying whole countries (like Bangladesh) and low-lying cities (London perhaps). And yet only four years before the UN team was saying the ice-sheet was secure for a thousand years. Second the acidification of the ocean from carbon dioxide threatens to destroy the whole food chain in the sea. Even in the short time since that Exeter meeting, there have been new warnings about the slowing down of the Gulf Stream[7] and the melting of the Himalayan glaciers.[8]

The human rights model has an emphasis on our species that makes it an unlikely bedfellow of the environmental movement. Neither the emphasis on civil and political rights nor on economic and social rights, much less the more recent notions of groups rights and the right to development,

---

[6] See M. McCarthy, 'Slouching towards Disaster' *The Tablet* 12 February 2005. [7] *Guardian* 1 December 2005.
[8] *Observer* 20 November 2005.

speak directly to the need to safeguard our natural resources, to pass on to our children a world that is at least as capable of sustaining them as it has us and our parents and grandparents. Indeed, sometimes the narrowness of the rights discourse, with its emphasis on property and privacy rights and due process for example, has proved itself positively inimical to environmental protection. How can we reconfigure the subject to make it fit with the greatest challenge the global community faces today, the threat of extinction at worst or of gravely reduced opportunities for many billions of people at best? The human rights idea has long emphasised the need to protect the vulnerable and the weak: who could be more vulnerable or weaker than those who have yet to be born? Our reckless destruction of the planet today comes at a cost to those who must try to live here tomorrow. It is an egregious example of the oppression by a transient majority (those alive today) of the huge numbers of people, as yet unborn, who must be given at least the same chance to lead good lives as we have had. The Preamble to the Universal Declaration of Human Rights notes that the document emerged as a response to a 'disregard and contempt for human rights' which had resulted 'in barbarous acts which have outraged the conscience of mankind', and that it was 'essential, if man is not to be compelled to have recourse, as a last resort, to rebellion against tyranny and oppression, that human rights should be protected by law'. But who is to represent the desires and wishes of those who may well in decades to come curse the conduct of our generation with the same venom as we now condemn the damage done by past generations of politically reckless zealots?

This reference to the environment reminds us that there are other issues apart from human rights which stand on the progressive side of politics and which attract strong support from the ethically-minded public. The human rights movement needs to build alliances with such groups, even if it requires a rethinking of basic attitudes. The environmental partnership for example might come at a cost of revising human rights attitudes to property ownership, due process and governmental regulation. The emphasis on human suffering which is so central to our subject makes collaboration with animal rights groups appear natural. But such a move should require us critically to reflect on the dubious specie-ism that is at our core. It might be time to return to John Locke's critique of the whole concept of a human species as a way of forging an alliance which does not require everything to be seen through the human eye. The raw fact of an animal suffering should be enough in itself to engender strong feelings of solidarity, and underpin joint campaigns against stag and fox hunting, dog-fighting and the like, without feeling the obligation to recast everything in human-rights-centred terms. There is also a difficult but important point to be made about the subjugation of animals that takes place under the guise of 'welfare' and 'the good life' – not the raising of animals for human consumption so much as the way pets are turned into instruments of their owner's will, specially bred purely for their novelty value for example or restricted in their life-chances simply to suit their owner's needs.[9]

---

[9] My thanks to Phil Scraton for making this point.

A natural alliance today – though historically admittedly an unlikely one – would be one between human rights and the progressive elements in the world's various religious movements. An unexpected development in these postmodern times has been a resurgence of interest in, and belief in the tenets of, the major world religions. The impulse that led successive generations of communities to tie their destiny to that of some unseen spiritual leader has proved itself to be a very deep one, and certainly not vulnerable to being destroyed by the rationalist project that we now describe as modernity. Indeed as John Gray has remarked, the secular ideologies that succeeded religion after the Enlightenment, Marxism and liberal humanism for example, were themselves essentially theological narratives in structure and function.[10] But the secularist perspective is said to have a 'worrying implication' – that without 'religion's insight that human beings are essentially flawed, we lose all checks on our hubristic pride, and risk making a false god of our own scientific genius.'[11] Of course in answering this critique the humanist and secularist alike can point to the civilising role of human rights, in other words the alternative ethic which this book has been all about. In doing so, he or she should be entirely open to building religious alliances. In a fascinating dialogue that he conducted with Cardinal Joseph Ratzinger (now Pope Benedict XVI) Jürgen Habermas remarked that in the face of the uprooting effects of technology and the global market, the

---

[10] See 'Torture: A Modest Proposal' in J. Gray, *Heresies. Against Progress and Other Illusions* (Granta Books, London, 2004).

[11] N. Buxton, 'Face to Faith' *Guardian* 19 November 2005.

liberal state should 'treat with care all cultural sources on which the normative consciousness and solidarity of citizens draws'.[12] I agree: humanitarian instincts are too precarious in global civil society to make it sensible to reject support from certain sources merely on account of quarrels in the distant past. This remains the case even if the content of human rights remains a source of radical dispute on certain core issues, such as the rights of homosexuals for example. Alliances can be strategic not all-encompassing, embracing an opponent on issue A (gay rights) in pursuit of success on issues B (world poverty) and C (environmental protection).

I end by returning to the threat of terrorism and what the human rights movement must do properly and adequately to confront it. Clearly it needs to stop being seen as devoted solely to cruel acts done by governmental power; this makes human rights advocates seem at times indifferent to subversive attacks and concerned only with state reactions. This is a tactical mistake. The movement needs to rebuild its relationship with the community as a whole and this means developing the kind of non-dogmatic relationship with democratic institutions that I talked about in chapter 3. There will always be a radical tension between human rights as a guarantee of individuated rights on the one hand and as a system of overarching values on the other. The pressures inherent in seeking to speak both specifically and generally at the same time are worked through in this complex inter-relationship between democracy and human rights, between a community dedicated to the success of all and the human rights impulse to

---

[12] See E. Skidelsky, 'Habermas vs the Pope' *Prospect* November 2005, p. 15.

insist that each of this 'all' should be individually esteemed. But this alliance should not be forged at any price, and we should be careful not to lose the sense of the particular, least we end up with human rights values that reflect majority intentions at the expense of the vulnerable.

The idea of human rights is a radical, emancipatory one. It should always be on the side of the underdog, perpetually trying to force an invisible individual or group of individuals into public view, giving them a language with which to shout for attention, and then having secured it to demand an end to suffering and a better set of life-chances. In the political world we now inhabit, the human rights language, this Esperanto of the virtuous as I called it in chapter 1, is the best way we have worked out of securing a hearing without killing in order to do so. In a world that upheld human rights values in a real way, terrorism would always be besides the point, a criminal waste of resources in every sense, rather than the cry for help from the voiceless that it has been in the past and sometimes is, even today.

Ahmed, A.S. *İslam under Siege. Living Dangerously in a Post-Honour World* (Polity Press, Cambridge, 2003)

Alston, P. (ed.) *Promoting Human Rights Through Bills of Rights. Comparative Perspectives* (Oxford University Press, Oxford, 1999)

Amnesty International Report 2005. *The State of the World's Human Rights* (London, 2005)

Anderson, G.W. (ed.) *Rights and Democracy: Essays in UK-Canadian Constitutionalism* (Blackstone Press, London, 1999)

Ashworth, A. *Human Rights, Serious Crime and Criminal Procedure* (Sweet and Maxwell, London, 2002)

Bamforth, N. and P. Leyland (eds.) *Public Law in a Multi-Layered Constitution* (Hart Publishing, 2003)

Barker, J. *The No-Nonsense Guide to Terrorism* (Verso Books, London, undated)

Batchelor, M. (ed.) *The Path of Compassion. The Bodhisattva Precepts* (Altamira Press, Walnut Creek, 2004)

Baxi, U. *The Future of Human Rights* (Oxford University Press, New Delhi, 2002)

Becker, J. *The Soviet Connection: State Sponsorship of Terrorism* (Institute for European and Defence and Strategic Studies, Occasional Paper No. 13, London, 1985)

Belden Fields, A. *Rethinking Human Rights for the New Millenium* (Palgrave Macmillan, New York, 2003)

Benedict XVI. *Deus Caritas Est.* Encyclical letter of Pope Benedict XVI, 25 December 2005.

Bennett, G. 'Legislative Responses to Terrorism: A View from Britain' 109 *Penn State Law Review* (2005) 947

Beyleveld, D. and R. Brownsword. 'Human Dignity, Human Rights, and Human Genetics' 61 *Modern Law Review* (1998) 661

Blom-Cooper, L. 'Third Party Intervention and Judicial Dissent' [2002] *Public Law* 602

Bobbio, N. *The Age of Rights* (Polity Press, Cambridge, 1996)

Bork, R.H. *The Tempting of America. The Political Seduction of the Law* (Sinclair-Stevenson, London, 1990)

Borradori, G. *Philosophy in a Time of Terror. Dialogues with Jürgen Habermas and Jacques Derrida* (The University of Chicago Press, Chicago and London, 2004)

Bright, M. 'Rendition: the Cover-Up' *New Statesman* 23 January 2006

Brysk, A. (ed.) *Globalization and Human Rights* (University of California Press, Berkeley, 2002)

Burnett, J. and D. Whyte. 'Embedded Expertise and the New Terrorism' [2005] *Journal for Crime, Conflict and Media Culture* 1

Cairneiro, R.L. (ed.) *The Evolution of Society. Selections from Herbert Spencer's Principles of Sociology* (University of Chicago Press, Chicago, 1967)

Cameron, I. 'Sweden' in C.A. Gearty (ed.), *European Civil Liberties and the European Convention on Human Rights* (Martinus Nijhoff, The Hague, 1997)

Campbell, T. 'Human Rights: A Culture of Controversy' 26 *Journal of Legal Studies* (1999) 6

Campbell, T., K.D. Ewing and A. Tomkins (eds.) *Sceptical Essays on Human Rights* (Oxford University Press, Oxford, 2001)

Campbell, T., J. Goldsworthy and A. Stone (eds.) *Protecting Human Rights. Instruments and Institutions* (Oxford University Press, Oxford, 2003)

Human Rights without a Bill of Rights: Institutional Performance and Reform in Australia (Ashgate, London, 2006 [in press])

Chandler, D. *From Kosovo to Kabul and Beyond. Human Rights and International Intervention* (Pluto Press, London, new edn 2006)

Clements, L. and P.A. Thomas. *Human Rights Act: A Success Story?* (Blackwell Publishing, Oxford, 2005)

Coady, T. and M. O'Keefe (eds.) *Terrorism and Justice. Moral Argument in a Threatened World* (Melbourne University Press, Melbourne, 2002)

Cranston, M. (ed.), *Jean-Jacques Rousseau, A Discourse on Inequality* (Penguin, Harmondsworth, 1984)

Danner, M. *Torture and Truth. America, Abu Ghraib and the War on Terror* (Granta Books, London, 2005)

Davies, O. 'Divine Silence, Human Rights' Aquinas Lecture 2005

Dershowitz, A.M. *Why Terrorism Works: Understanding the Threat, Responding to the Challenge* (Yale University Press, New Haven, 2002)

Dicey, A.V. *Lectures Introductory to a Study of the Law of the Constitution* (Macmillan, London, 2nd edn 1885)

Donnelly, J. *Universal Human Rights in Theory and Practice* (Cornell University Press, Ithaca and London, 2nd edn 2003)

Douzinas, C. 'Human Rights and Postmodern Utopia' 11 *Law and Critique* (2000) 219

The End of Human Rights (Hart Publishing, Oxford, 2000)

Duffy, H. *The 'War on Terror' and the Framework of International Law* (Cambridge University Press, Cambridge, 2005)

Dunn, J. *Locke: A Very Short Introduction* (Oxford University Press, Oxford, 2003)

Dunne, T. and N.J. Wheeler (eds.) *Human Rights in Global Politics* (Cambridge University Press, Cambridge, 1999)

Dworkin, R. *Taking Rights Seriously* (Gerald Duckworth & Co, London, 1978)

'Rights as Trumps' in J. Waldron (ed.), *Theories of Rights* (Oxford University Press, Oxford, 1984)

Epp, C.R. *The Rights Revolution. Lawyers, Activists, and Supreme Courts in Comparative Perspective* (University of Chicago Press, Chicago, 1998)

Ewing, K.D. 'The Bill of Rights Debate: Democracy or Juristocracy in Britain' in K.D. Ewing, C.A. Gearty and B.A. Hepple (eds.), *Human Rights and Labour Law* (Mansell, London, 1994)
'The Futility of the Human Rights Act' [2004] *Public Law* 829

Ewing, K.D. and C.A. Gearty, *Freedom under Thatcher. Civil Liberties in Modern Britain* (Oxford University Press, Oxford, 1990)
Democracy or a Bill of Rights (Society of Labour Lawyers, London, 1991)
The Struggle for Civil Liberties (Oxford University Press, Oxford, 2000)

Ewing, K.D., C.A. Gearty and B.A. Hepple (eds.), *Human Rights and Labour Law* (Mansell, London, 1994)

Feinberg, J. *Rights, Justice and the Bounds of Liberty. Essays in Social Philosophy* (Princeton University Press, New Jersey, 1980)

Feldman, D. 'Human Dignity as a Legal Value' [1999] *Public Law* 682

Fenwick, H. *Civil Rights: New Labour, Freedom and the Human Rights Act* (Longman, Harlow, 2000)

Filibeck, G. *Human Rights in the Teaching of the Church: From John XXIII to John Paul II* (Libreria Editrice Vaticana, Vatican City, 1994)

Finnis, J. *Natural Law and Natural Rights* (Clarendon Press, Oxford, 1980)

Fisk, R. *Pity the Nation: Lebanon at War* (A. Deutsch, London, 1990)

Forsythe, D.P. *Human Rights and Peace. International and National Dimensions* (University of Nebraska Press, Lincoln, 1993)

Francis, S.T. *The Soviet Strategy of Terror* (The Heritage Foundation, Washington DC, 1981).

Freeman, C. *The Closing of the Western Mind. The Rise of Faith and the Fall of Reason* (William Heinemann, London, 2002)

Gallagher, M.P. 'Struggle and Conversion' *The Tablet* 10 September 2005

Gearty, C.A. *Terror* (Faber and Faber, London, 1991).

'The Paradox of United States Democracy' 26 *University of Richmond Law Review* (1992) 259

'Political Violence and Civil Liberties' in C. McCrudden and G. Chambers (eds.) *Individual Rights and the Law in Britain* (The Law Society and Clarendon Press, Oxford, 1994) ch. 5

'Democracy and Human Rights in the European Court of Human Rights: A Critical Appraisal' 51 *Northern Ireland Law Quarterly Review* (2000) 381

'Terrorism and Morality' [2003] *European Human Rights Law Review* 377

Principles of Human Rights Adjudication (Oxford University Press, Oxford, 2004)

'11 September 2001, Counter-terrorism and the Human Rights Act' 32 *Journal of Legal Studies* (2005) 18

'Human Rights in an Age of Counter-Terrorism: Injurious, Irrelevant or Indispensable?' 58 *Current Legal Problems* (2005) 25

'With a Little Help From Our Friends' (2005) 34 *Index on Censorship* 36

Gearty, C.A. (ed.) *European Civil Liberties and the European Convention on Human Rights* (Martinus Nijhoff, The Hague, 1997)

Gearty, C.A. and A. Tomkins (eds.) *Understanding Human Rights* (Mansell Publishing Ltd, London, 1996)

Gewirth, A. *Human Rights. Essays on Justification and Applications* (University of Chicago Press, Chicago, 1982)

Glendon, M.A. *Rights Talk. The Impoverishment of Political Discourse* (The Free Press, New York, 1991)

Golder, B. and G. Williams. 'What is "Terrorism"? Problems of Legal Definition' 27 *University of New South Wales Law Journal* (2004) 270

Goren, R. *The Soviet Union and Terrorism* (Allen and Unwin, London, 1984)

Gray, J. 'Torture: A Modest Proposal' in J. Gray, *Heresies. Against Progress and Other Illusions* (Granta Books, London, 2004)

Greenberg, K.J. 'Secrets and Lies' *The Nation* 26 December 2005

Grey, T.C. 'Holmes and Legal Pragmatism' 41 *Stanford Law Review* (1988–89) 787

Griffin, J. 'Discrepancies Between the Best Philosophical Account of Human Rights and the International Law of Human Rights' *Proceedings of the Aristotelian Society* (2001)
'First Steps in an Account of Human Rights' 9 *European Journal of Philosophy* (2001) pp. 306–27

Griffith, J.A.G. 'The Political Constitution' 42 *Modern Law Review* (1979) 1

Guelke, A. *The Age of Terrorism and the International Political System* (Tauris Academic Studies, I.B. Tauris Publishers, London, 1995)

Gutteridge, W. (ed.) *The New Terrorism* (Mansell Publishers, London, 1986)

Hacker, P.M.S. *Wittgenstein on Human Nature* (Orion Publishing Group, London, 1997)

Hannett, S. 'Third Party Interventions: In the Public Interest?' [2003] *Public Law* 128

Harlow, C. 'The Political Constitution Reworked' [2006] *New Zealand Law Review* [in press]

Hayden, P. *The Philosophy of Human Rights* (Paragon House, St Paul Minnesota, 2001)

Hills, J. *Inequality and the State* (Oxford University Press, Oxford, 2004)

Hirschl, R. *Towards Juristocracy. The Origins and Consequences of the New Constitutionalism* (Harvard University Press, Cambridge Mass., 2004)

Hoge Jr., J.F. and G. Rose, *Understanding the War on Terror* (Council on Foreign Relations, New York, 2005)

Holmes, S. 'The War of the Liberals' *The Nation* 14 November 2005

Holmes, S. and C.R. Sunstein. *The Cost of Rights. Why Liberty Depends on Taxes* (W.W. Norton and Co, New York, 1999)

Human Rights Watch, *World Report 2006* (Human Rights Watch and Seven Stories Press, New York, 2006).

Hunt, M. *Using Human Rights Law in English Courts* (Hart Publishing, Oxford, 1997)

Huntingdon, S. 'The Clash of Civilizations' (1993) 72 *Foreign Affairs* 22

Ignatieff, M. *The Lesser Evil. Political Ethics in an Age of Terror* (Edinburgh University Press, Edinburgh, 2004)

Ishay, M.R. *The Human Rights Reader* (Routledge, New York, 1997)
The History of Human Rights. From Ancient Times to the Globalization Era (University of California Press, Berkeley, California, 2004)

Ison, T. 'The Sovereignty of the Judiciary' 10 *Adelaide Law Review* (1985) 3

Jacob, J.M. *The Republican Crown. Layers and the Making of the State in Twentieth Century Britain* (Dartmouth, Aldershot, 1996)

James, W. *The Varieties of Religious Experience. A Study in Human Nature* (Penguin Books, New York, 1985)

Joint Committee on Human Rights, Second Report, *Anti-terrorism, Crime and Security Bill* HL (2001–2002) 37, HC (2001–2002) 372; Fifth Report, *Anti-terrorism, Crime and Security Bill: Further Report* HL (2001–2002) 51, HC (2001–2002) 420.

Klang, M. and A. Murray (eds.) *Human Rights in the Digital Age* (London, Glasshouse Press, Cavendish Publishing, 2005)

Klein, N. ' "Never Before!" Our Amnesiac Torture Debate' *The Nation*, 26 December 2005

Klug, F. *Values for a Godless Age. The Story of the United Kingdom's New Bill of Rights* (Penguin Books, London, 2000)

Kramer, M.H., N.E. Simmonds and H. Steiner. *A Debate over Rights. Philosophical Inquiries* (Clarendon Press, Oxford, 1998)

Laqueur, W. *The Age of Terrorism* (Weidenfeld and Nicolson, London, 1987)

Langlois, A.J. 'Human Rights without Democracy? A Critique of the Separationist Thesis' 25 *Human Rights Quarterly* (2003) 990

Laski, H. *Liberty in the Modern State* (Faber and Faber, London, 1930)

Layard, R. *Happiness. Lessons from a New Science* (Allen Lane, London, 2005)

Levinson, S. (ed.) *Torture. A Collection* (Oxford University Press, Oxford, 2004)

Lewis, A. 'The Torture Administration' *The Nation*, 26 December 2005

Lloyd of Berwick, Lord. *Inquiry into Legislation Against Terrorism* (1996, Cm. 3420, Chair: Lord Lloyd of Berwick)

Lomas, O.G. 'The Executive and the Anti-Terrorist Legislation of 1939' [1980] *Public Law* 16

Loughlin, M. 'Rights Discourse and Public Law Thought in the United Kingdom' in G.W. Anderson (ed.) *Rights and Democracy: Essays in UK-Canadian Constitutionalism* (Blackstone Press, London, 1999)

'Rights, Democracy and Law' in T. Campbell, K.D. Ewing and A. Tomkins (eds.) *Sceptical Essays on Human Rights* (Oxford University Press, Oxford, 2001)

Luttwak, E. *The Grand Strategy of the Soviet Union* (Weidenfeld and Nicolson, London, 1983)

Lyons, G.M. and J. Mayall (eds.) *International Human Rights in the 21st Century. Protecting the Rights of Groups* (Rowman and Littlefield Publishers Inc, Lanham, 2003)

McCarthy, M. 'Slouching towards Disaster' *The Tablet* 12 February 2005

McCrudden, C. and G. Chambers (eds.) *Individual Rights and the Law in Britain* (The Law Society and Clarendon Press, Oxford, 1994)

McDonald, L. 'New Directions in the Australian Bill of Rights Debate' [2004] *Public Law* 22

MacIntyre, A. *After Virtue. A Study in Moral Theory* (Duckworth, London, 2nd edn 1985)

Macpherson, C.B. *The Political Theory of Possessive Individualism* (Oxford University Press, Oxford, 1962)

Mahoney, J. *The Challenge of Human Rights* (Blackwell Publishing, Oxford, 2006 [in press])

Mandel, M. *The Charter of Rights and the Legalization of Politics in Canada* (Thompson Educational Press, Toronto, 2nd edn 1994)
'A Brief History of the New Constitutionalism, or "How We Changed Everything so that Everything Would Remain the Same"' 32 *Israel Law Review* (1998) 250

Miller, D. (ed.) *Liberty* (Oxford University Press, Oxford, 1991)

Netanyahu, B. *Fighting Terrorism. How Democracies Can Defeat Domestic and International Terrorists* (Allison and Busby Ltd, London, 1996)

Netanyahu, B. (ed.) *Terrorism: How the West Can Win* (Weidenfeld and Nicolson, London, 1986)

Nino, C.S. *The Ethics of Human Rights* (Clarendon Press, Oxford, 1991)

Norman, R. *The Moral Philosophers: An Introduction to Ethics* (Clarendon Press, Oxford, 1983)

Nussbaum, M. *Upheavals of Thought: The Intelligence of Emotions* (Cambridge University Press, Cambridge, 2001)

Nystrom, D. and K. Puckett, *Against Bosses, Against Oligarchies: A Conversation with Richard Rorty* (Prickly Pear Pamphlets, Charlottesville, Virginia, 1998)

Oberleitner, G. 'A Just War Against Terror' 16 *Peace Review* (2004) 263

O'Neill, O. *A Question of Trust* (Cambridge University Press, Cambridge, 2002)

Pascal, B. *Pascal's Pensées* (Everyman Library, London, 1956)

Perry, M.J. *The Idea of Human Rights. Four Inquiries* (Oxford University Press, New York, 1998)

Plant, R. *Politics, Theology and History* (Cambridge University Press, Cambridge, 2001)

Ra'anan, U., R.L. Pfaltzgraff, R.H. Schultz, E. Halperin and I. Lukes, *Hydra of Carnage* (Lexington Books, Lexington, 1986)

Rawls, J. 'The Domain of Political and Overlapping Consensus' 64 *New York University Law Review* (1989) no. 2

Raz, J. 'Right-Based Moralities' in J. Waldron (ed.) *Theories of Rights* (Oxford University Press, Oxford, 1984)

Ridley, M. *The Origins of Virtue* (Penguin Books, London, 1996)

Rorty, R. *Contingency, Irony, and Solidarity* (Cambridge University Press, Cambridge, 1989)

Philosophy and Social Hope (Penguin Books, London, 1999)

'Human Rights, Rationality and Sentimentality' in S. Shute and S. Hurley (eds.) *On Human Rights* (Basic Books, New York, 1993)

'Post Democracy' 26 *London Review of Books* (2004) no. 7 (1 April)

Rose, D. *Guantanamo. America's War on Human Rights* (Faber and Faber, London, 2004)

Roth, K. and M. Worden (eds.) *Torture. Does It Make Us Safer? Is it Ever Ok?* (The New Press, Human Rights Watch, New York, 2005)

Sands, P. *Lawless World. America and the Making and Breaking of Global Rules* (Allen Lane, London, 2005)

Sarat, A. and T.R. Kearns, *Human Rights. Concepts, Contests, Contingencies* (University of Michigan Press, Ann Arbor, 2002)

Schwartz, B. *A History of the Supreme Court* (Oxford University Press, New York and Oxford, 1993)

Sedley, S. *Freedom, Law and Justice* (Sweet and Maxwell, London, 1999)

'Are Human Rights Universal, and Does It Matter?' The Holdsworth Lecture, University of Birmingham, 25 November 2005

Sellars, K. *The Rise and Rise of Human Rights* (Sutton Publishing, Stroud, 2002)

Sen, A. 'Elements of a Theory of Human Rights' 32 *Philosophy and Public Affairs* (2004) 315

Shaw, M. *International Law* (Cambridge University Press, Cambridge, 5th edn 2003)

Shute, S. and S. Hurley (eds.) *On Human Rights* (Basic Books, New York)

Sieghart, P. *The Lawful Rights of Mankind* (Oxford University Press, Oxford, 1986)

Simpson, A.W.B. *Human Rights and the End of Empire. Britain and the Genesis of the European Convention* (Oxford University Press, Oxford, 2001)

Singh, R. *The Future of Human Rights in the United Kingdom. Essays on Law and Practice* (Hart Publishing, Oxford, 1997)

Skidelsky, E. 'Habermas vs the Pope' *Prospect* November 2005

Smith, R. 'Test Case Strategies and the Human Rights Act' 1 *Justice Journal* (2004) 65

Sniderman, P.M., J.F. Fletcher, P.H. Russell and P.E. Tetlock. *The Clash of Rights. Liberty, Equality and Legitimacy in Pluralist Democracy* (Yale University Press, New Haven, 1996)

Sontag, S. *Regarding the Pain of Others* (Penguin Books, London, 2003)

Sterling, C. *The Terror Network: the Secret War of International Terrorism* (Weidenfeld and Nicolson, London, 1981)

Tasioulas, J. 'Human Rights, Universality and the Values of Personhood: Retracing Griffin's Steps' 10 *European Journal of Philosophy* (2002) 79

Tomkins, A. *Public Law* (Oxford University Press, Oxford, 2003)

Tushnet, M. 'Living with a Bill of Rights' in C. Gearty and A. Tomkins (eds.) *Understanding Human Rights* (Mansell Publishing Ltd, London, 1996)

Taking the Constitution Away from the Courts (Princeton University Press, Princeton New Jersey, 1999)

United Nations. *International Cooperation at a Crossroads: Aid, Trade and Security in an Unequal World* (UNDP Human Development Report, Oxford University Press, 2005)

United Nations High Level Panel. *A More Secure World: Our Shared Responsibility. Report of the High Level Panel on Threats, Challenges and Change* (UN, A/59/565, December 2004)

Vanden Eynde, M. 'Reflections on Martha Nussbaum's Work on Compassion from a Buddhist Perspective' 11 *Journal of Buddhist Ethics* (2004) 46

Wadham, J. *Blackstone's Guide to The Human Rights Act 1998* (Oxford University Press, Oxford, 3rd edn 2003)

Waldron, J. (ed.) *'Nonsense upon Stilts': Bentham, Burke and Marx on the Rights of Man* (Metheun, London, 1987)

Theories of Rights (Oxford University Press, Oxford, 1984)

Ward, I. *Introduction to Critical Legal Theory* (Cavendish Publishing Ltd, London, 2nd edn 2004)

Wardlaw, G. *Political Terrorism: Theory, Tactics and Counter-Measures* (Cambridge University Press, Cambridge, 2nd edn 1989)

Webber, J. 'A Modest (but Robust) Defence of Statutory Bills of Rights'' in T. Campbell, J. Goldsworthy and A. Stone (eds.) *Human Rights without a Bill of Rights: Institutional Performance and Reform in Australia* (Ashgate, London, 2006 [in press])

Williams, G. *A Bill of Rights for Australia* (University of New South Wales Press, Sydney, 2000).

Human Rights under the Australian Constitution (Oxford University Press, Melbourne, 2002)

Wilson, R.A. *Human Rights in the 'War on Terror'* (Cambridge University Press, Cambridge, 2005)

INDEX

Abu Ghraib, 134, 138, 142
Abu Nidhal, 119, 120
Afghanistan, 123, 128, 134, 135
Al Qaeda, 102, 104, 120, 122, 133
Alito, Samuel A., 87
Amnesty International, 113
Aquinas, Thomas, 44
Arafat, Yasser, 115, 121
asylum seekers, 67
Australia, 65

Bentham, Jeremy, 21, 24, 25, 28, 51,
     76, 94–95
bills of rights
     dangers of legalism, 4, 62–70
     growth, 8, 63–64
     models, 92–93
Bin Laden, Osama, 120
Blackmun, Harry, 85–86
Blair, Tony, 88, 102, 106
Bork, Robert, 87
Bratza, Nicholas, 88
Burke, Edmund, 24, 25, 28
Bush, George W., 87, 127, 129,
     132

Cameron, David, 27
Canadian Charter of Rights, 64,
     92–93, 96
Cheney, Dick, 132
China, 145

compassion, 43–50, 60
Council of Europe, 138
counter-terrorism
     See also terrorism
     19th century, 99–100
     challenging human rights,
          102–109
     crisis, 12–14
     dictators' enthusiasm for, 113
     and human rights, 123–135
     human rights cloak, 13, 134–135,
          143
     human rights fight-back, 136–139
     and intellectuals, 130–135
     redefinition of human rights,
          108
     UK detention without trial,
          96–97, 103, 104
     UK responses to terror, 99–109,
          125–126
     UK rushed legislation, 105–106
     US disregard of human rights,
          90–91, 107, 127–133
     vague crimes, 104–105
Cromwell, Oliver, 105

Darwin, Charles, 29, 31, 40–41,
     49–50, 57–58
Davies, Oliver, 43–44, 48–49
Davis, David, 95
democracy, 50, 55, 76–77, 79, 80–86

INDEX